THE LAW OF PERSONAL INJURY

2nd Edition

by
Margaret C. Jasper

Oceana's Legal Almanac Series
Law for the Layperson

2000
Oceana Publications, Inc.
Dobbs Ferry, New York

Library of Congress Control Number: 00-134130

ISBN 0-379-11344-9

Oceana's Legal Almanac Series: Law for the Layperson
ISSN 1075-7376

©2000 by Oceana Publications, Inc.

Manufactured in the United States of America on acid-free paper.

To My Husband Chris

Your love and support
are my motivation and inspiration

-and-

In memory of my son, Jimmy

Table of Contents

CHAPTER 2:
A PERSONAL INJURY FACT PATTERN

CHAPTER 3:
PREMISES LIABILITY

CHAPTER 4:
ASSAULT AND BATTERY

CHAPTER 9:
LIABILITY AND DAMAGES

CHAPTER 10:
FINAL RESOLUTION

APPENDICES

ABOUT THE AUTHOR

MARGARET C. JASPER is an attorney engaged in the general practice of law in South Salem, New York, concentrating in the areas of personal injury and entertainment law. Ms. Jasper holds a Juris Doctor degree from Pace University School of Law, White Plains, New York, is a member of the New York and Connecticut bars, and is certified to practice before the United States District Courts for the Southern and Eastern Districts of New York, and the United States Supreme Court.

Ms. Jasper has been appointed to the panel of arbitrators of the American Arbitration Association and the law guardian panel for the Family Court of the State of New York, is a member of the Association of Trial Lawyers of America, and is a New York State licensed real estate broker and member of the Westchester County Board of Realtors, operating as Jasper Real Estate, in South Salem, New York.

Ms. Jasper is the author and general editor of the following legal almanacs: Juvenile Justice and Children's Law; Marriage and Divorce; Estate Planning; The Law of Contracts; The Law of Dispute Resolution; Law for the Small Business Owner; The Law of Personal Injury; Real Estate Law for the Homeowner and Broker; Everyday Legal Forms; Dictionary of Selected Legal Terms; The Law of Medical Malpractice; The Law of Product Liability; The Law of No-Fault Insurance; The Law of Immigration; The Law of Libel and Slander; The Law of Buying and Selling; Elder Law; The Right to Die; AIDS Law; The Law of Obscenity and Pornography; The Law of Child Custody; The Law of Debt Collection; Consumer Rights Law; Bankruptcy Law for the Individual Debtor; Victim's Rights Law; Animal Rights Law; Workers' Compensation Law; Employee Rights in the Workplace; Probate Law; Environmental Law; Labor Law; The Americans with Disabilities Act; The Law of Capital Punishment; Education Law; The Law of Violence Against Women; Landlord-Tenant Law; Insurance Law; Religion and the Law; Commercial Law; Motor Vehicle Law; Social Security Law; The Law of Drunk Driving; The Law of Speech and the First Amendment;

Employment Discrimination Under Title VII; Hospital Liability Law; Home Mortgage Law Primer; Copyright Law; Patent Law; Trademark Law; Special Education Law; Premises Liability Law; and The Law of Attachment and Garnishment.

INTRODUCTION

This legal almanac explores the area of law known generally as "personal injury." Personal injury law involves "tortious conduct"—that is, conduct which is wrongful. Thus, personal injury law is also known as the law of torts. The actor who performed the wrongful conduct is known as a tortfeasor.

This almanac covers the general aspects of the three major areas of liability in personal injury law: negligence, strict liability, and intentional torts. The subtopics of premises liability; assault; medical malpractice; product liability; and defamation are also explored.

Both medical malpractice and product liability are hybrid actions in that a complaint may contain allegations of negligence, intentional tort and strict liability. Further, medical malpractice is subject to special rules not required in a standard negligence action.

The almanac also sets forth a personal injury fact pattern encompassing six common personal injury claims, and the elements of a prima facie case for each of those claims are explored.

The law discussed in this Almanac applies in most jurisdictions, and the applicable section of the Restatement of Torts is set forth where helpful to a better understanding. However, readers are cautioned, when researching a particular problem, not to rely on a general discussion of the law, but to always check the law of their own jurisdictions.

The Appendix provides sample documents, applicable statutes, and other pertinent information and data. The Glossary contains definitions of many of the terms used throughout the almanac.

CHAPTER 1:
OVERVIEW OF PERSONAL INJURY LAW

THE HISTORY OF TORT LAW

Common Law Torts

In thirteenth and fourteenth century England, causes of action for tortious conduct could only be brought in the King's court if a person broke one of the King's writs. The commission of a tort was considered a semi-criminal act. The plaintiff sought compensation, and the defendant had to appear or go to jail. The most common tort cause of action at that time involved trespass, of which there were four classifications:

(1) Trespass "vi et armis"—This cause of action referred to trespass by force of arms.

(2) Trespass "de bonis asportates"—This cause of action involved the taking of the plaintiff's property.

(3) Trespass "quare clauson frogit"—This cause of action involved the trespass onto the plaintiff's property. Damages were presumed, and the plaintiff did not have to show negligence or intent, but merely had to show that there was an application of direct force.

(4) Trespass "on the case"—This cause of action was used where the harm resulted from an indirect application of force, with or without intent. In this case, damages had to be shown. Trespass on the case evolved into a cause of action for direct or indirect harm involving damages that were not intended because they resulted from either accident or negligence.

Modern Day Tort Law

Our modern day tort law is largely derived from the English Common Law. The common law refers to the body of law which is derived from court decisions. Those decisions—known as precedents—are followed by other judges in cases with similar circumstances so as to establish some consistency in the law. This is known as the doctrine of stare decisis.

A departure from a precedent may occur if it can be shown that there is a good reason to change the law. Nevertheless, statutory law, which is made by our elected officials, supersedes the common law, and can change precedent. Personal injury law is derived from both the common law and the statutory law.

BASES OF LIABILITY

As set forth below, there are three main bases of liability in personal injury law: (1) negligence; (2) strict liability; and (3) intentional torts.

Negligence

Negligence encompasses unintentionally caused harms. Negligence is the most important basis of tort liability in the United States. The basis of liability is the creation of an unreasonable risk of harm to another. Common negligence actions include premises liability claims and automobile accident claims. While primarily negligence actions, medical malpractice claims and product liability claims may also involve allegations of negligence, intentional tort and strict liability. All of these claims are discussed more fully in this almanac.

Risk of Harm

An actor who causes harm is not held liable in negligence simply because his activity involves a risk of harm to others, such as driving a car or flying a plane. For negligence to be found, the actor's conduct must involve a risk of harm greater than society is willing to accept in light of the benefits to be derived from that activity. That is, the risk must be unreasonable.

Case law has held that an actor is not liable for injury unless it was intentionally or negligently caused. Consequently, the loss from an unavoidable accident will remain with the plaintiff unless negligence or intentional harm can be proven. The plaintiff bears the burden of proof.

The Reasonable Person Standard

The general standard in most negligence cases is that the actor used reasonable care under the circumstances. The ultimate question is not simply whether a reasonable person would have recognized the risk he was creating, but whether recognizing the risk, that person would have acted differently. The duty of a reasonable person is a function of three variables:

(1) the probability that the harm will occur;

(2) the gravity of the resulting injury if it does occur; and

(3) the burden of adequate cautions to prevent the harm.

Thus, liability depends on whether the burden of adequate precaution is less than the probability of harm occurring, multiplied by the gravity of the injury if the harm does occur.

The Restatement of Torts defines an unreasonable act as one which a reasonable man would recognize as involving a risk of harm to another. The general rule states that the risk is unreasonable, and the act negligent, if the risk is of such magnitude as to outweigh what the law regards as the utility of the act, or of the particular manner in which it is accomplished.

The factors to be considered in determining the utility of the actor's conduct are:

(1) the social value of the interest to be advanced or protected by the conduct;

(2) the extent of chance that the interest will be advanced or protected by the conduct; and

(3) the extent of chance that such interest can be adequately advanced or protected by another less dangerous course of conduct.

The factors to be considered in determining the magnitude of the risk are:

(1) the social value of the interest imperiled;

(2) the chance that the actor's conduct will cause an invasion of interest of another or another's class;

(3) the extent of harm likely to be caused to the interest imperiled; and

(4) the number of persons whose interests are likely to be invaded if the risk takes effect in harm.

The Emergency Doctrine

In an emergency situation, when one must act before having time to think, instinctive action cannot be said to be careless unless the actor is unfit to act in such an emergency. An exception exists in that the person who negligently causes the emergency cannot invoke the emergency doctrine to escape liability.

The Elements of a Negligence Cause of Action

The elements of a negligence cause of action which must be proved include: (1) a duty; (2) a breach of that duty; (3) foreseeability; (4) proximate cause—that is, the breach caused the harm; and (5) a resulting injury.

Duty

Duty is defined as that degree of ordinary care owed to another under the circumstances. Ordinary care is the care a prudent and cautious person would take in the same situation. The plaintiff bears the burden of proving that the defendant acted without ordinary care. The defendant has the burden of proving contributory negligence on the part of the plaintiff.

Modification of the Ordinary Care Standard

The general standard of ordinary care is modified where there exists a special relationship between the parties. For example:

1. Landowners owe a duty depending on the classification of persons on the land as either trespassers, licensees, or invitees. Licensees and invitees are owed a higher standard of care because they have permission to be on the land. The lowest duty of care is owed to a trespasser.

2. Common carriers have the duty to use reasonable care to assist passengers in distress.

3. Hospital emergency room personnel are under a duty to treat indigent patients. Thus, private hospitals should at least stabilize a person before transferring the person to a municipal hospital.

4. Ship captains have a duty to rescue crewpersons, passengers, etc.

5. Certain governmental employees, such as police officers and fire fighters, have a duty to rescue.

6. A doctor or psychotherapist treating a mentally ill patient bears a duty to use reasonable care to give threatened persons such warnings as are essential to avert foreseeable danger arising from the patient's condition or treatment. This is also an exception to the client-patient confidentiality doctrine.

Breach of Duty

Once it has been established that there is a relationship between the parties in which a duty has arisen, it must be shown that the defendant breached that duty in some manner.

Foreseeability

Further, in order for the individual to be deemed negligent, there is a common law requirement that it is foreseeable that his conduct created the danger. The risk of injury to the third party must have been foreseeable for the actor to be held responsible. If a reasonable prudent person could not have foreseen the probability that injury would occur as a result of his conduct, there is no negligence and no liability.

Proximate Cause

The plaintiff must further prove that the foreseeable injury sustained as a result of the breach of duty were proximately caused by the negligent act or omission of the defendant. The act is a proximate cause of the injury if it was a substantial factor in bringing about the injury, and without which the result would not have occurred.

The tests used by the courts to determine whether proximate cause exists are the "but for" and the "substantial factor" test. The "but for" test asks the question: Would the injury not have occurred "but for" the negligence of the defendant? If the answer is yes, then proximate cause exists. The "substantial factor" test is used when the fact pattern is more complicated and there exists more than one cause for the plaintiff's injury. In that case, proximate cause exists for all of the acts or omissions which were substantial factors in bringing about the injury, and without which the injury would not have occurred.

Special Rules Governing Proof in Negligence Cases

There are certain special rules relating to the introduction of proof in negligence cases. These rules govern introduction of:

(1) the violation of criminal statutes;

(2) custom;

(3) expert testimony; and

(4) the doctrine of res ipsa loquitur.

Violation of Criminal Statutes

In certain cases, the violation of a criminal statute may be proof of a violation of the requisite standard of care in the civil case. The plaintiff must show a connection between the statutory violation and the harm suffered to prove negligence. In other words, there must be causation.

For example, the unauthorized practice of medicine is a criminal violation. New York has a statute providing that in any action for damages for personal injuries or death against a person not authorized to practice medicine, when such unauthorized acts are a proximate or contributing cause of the injuries or death, the unauthorized practice of medicine shall be deemed prima facie evidence of negligence.

In determining whether the violation of a statute may be applied as proof of negligence, there are two questions which should be asked:

(1) Is the injured person within the class of persons who are protected by statute from suffering a certain injury? and

(2) Is the particular injury the statute seeks to prevent the same injury the plaintiff has suffered?

If the answer to both questions is yes, then the violation of that statute may be introduced as evidence of the wrongdoer's negligence.

Further, the violation of a safety statute—one which is made in the interest of the general public and which defines the degree of care to be used under specific conditions—creates a rebuttable presumption that the actor was negligent. Violation of such a statute is known as negligence per se.

Custom

One is not ordinarily considered negligent in connection with acts that conform to a common practice if that practice has existed for years without resulting in any injury and nothing about the practice shows a want of due care. For example, in a medical malpractice case, as more fully discussed in Chapter 5, the plaintiff must prove that the defendant failed to exercise that degree of skill, care, and learning possessed by other persons in the same profession in order to recover.

Expert Testimony

Expert witnesses are asked questions requiring testimony that is beyond lay knowledge. If the information is highly technical, expert witnesses are permitted to draw a conclusion. However, concerning matters which the jury can understand, an expert witness is not permitted to draw his legal conclusion or opinion and render it to the jury.

The Doctrine of Res Ipsa Loquitur

"Res Ipsa Loquitur" is Latin for "the thing speaks for itself." This doctrine allows a plaintiff to be victorious in certain cases when there is a gap in the evidence which prevents the plaintiff from proving the defendant's specific negligent conduct. Most states permit, but do not compel, an inference of negligence in such a case.

There are two foundations for application of the doctrine of res ipsa loquitur:

(1) There must be exclusive control and management by the defendant of the instrument which caused the injury, and the plaintiff must not have contributed to the accident.

(2) The accident could not have happened without the absence of due care by the defendant.

The defendant must rebut the inference of negligence by showing that he exercised due care.

Strict Liability

The three most common areas in which strict liability arises are: (1) abnormally dangerous activities; (2) animal ownership; and (3) product liability. Product liability actions are unique in that the claim may involve aspects of strict liability, negligence, and intentional torts all in one action. Product liability law is discussed more fully in this almanac.

Abnormally Dangerous Activities

An abnormally dangerous activity is defined in Section 520 of the Restatement of Torts, as follows:

In determining whether an activity is abnormally dangerous, the following factors are to be considered:

(a) Whether the activity involves a high degree of risk of some harm to the person, land or chattels of others;

(b) Whether the gravity of the harm which may result from it is likely to be great;

(c) Whether the risk cannot be eliminated by the exercise of reasonable care;

(d) Whether the activity is not a matter of common usage;

(e) Whether the activity is inappropriate to the place where it is carried on; and

(f) The value of the activity to the community.

If the use was obvious and natural, given the circumstances, then any damages caused thereby must be based in negligence rather than strict liability.

Thus, strict liability could be imposed for any damages caused by a non-natural use of a property, which use is extraordinary or unusual, as set forth in Section 519 of the Restatement of Torts:

(1) One who carries on an abnormally dangerous activity is subject to liability for harm to the person, land or chattels of another resulting from the activity, although he has exercised the utmost care to prevent such harm.

(2) Such strict liability is limited to the kind of harm the risk of which makes the activity abnormally dangerous. Such use depends on the circumstances and the past experience of the particular use. If it has been an established usage, although possibly non-natural, it would not impose strict liability if the damage was caused thereby.

Animal Ownership

The earliest cases at common law, which imposed strict liability on the owners of animals, were trespass cases. Owners were held liable for the harm caused to property by wandering livestock. The rule that the owner of trespassing livestock is strictly liable for such harm is firmly established today and has been adopted in Section 504 of the Restatement of Torts:

> (1) A possessor of livestock which intrude upon the land of another is liable for their intrusion and for any harm done while upon the land to its possessor or a member of his household, although the possessor of the livestock exercised the utmost care to prevent them from intruding.

Section 504 also provides an example of contributory negligence of the plaintiff:

> (4) A possessor of land who by the common law applicable to that part of the state in which the land is situated, or by statute, is required to fence his land to prevent the intrusion of the livestock, is barred from recovery against the possessors of intruding livestock if he fails to erect and maintain the required fence.

Although wild animals are not considered livestock under Restatement Section 504, owners and possessors of wild animals are strictly liable for harm, including personal injuries, caused by their animals' escape. Nevertheless, zoo employees are liable only for their own negligence.

The owner of a domesticated animal will be liable to injured persons only if the owner knows of the vicious tendencies of the animal, as set forth in Section 509 of the Restatement of Torts:

> (1) A possessor of a domestic animal which he knows or has reason to know has dangerous propensities abnormal to its class, is subject to liability for harm done by the animal to others, even though he has exercised the utmost care to prevent such harm.

> (2) Such liability is limited to harm which results from the abnormal dangerous propensity of which the possessor knows or has reason to know.

Of course, if a dog owner is negligent in failing to control or confine his animal, he will be liable for negligence whether or not he is aware of a vicious or dangerous propensity sufficient to hold the owner strictly liable. Nevertheless, there are a number of defenses available to dog owners, even when the plaintiff sues in strict liability. The most common of these defenses is provocation on the part of the plaintiff.

Intentional Torts

An intentional tort differs from an act of negligence in that—as the name implies—an intentional tort requires the element of intent. Common intentional tort claims include assault and battery and defamation. Each intentional tort has very specific elements which must be proven in order to establish a prima facie case. The elements of the intentional torts of defamation and assault and battery are discussed in this almanac.

THE STATUTE OF LIMITATIONS

In general, a statute of limitation refers to any law which sets forth a time period within which a claimant must bring a lawsuit to avoid being barred from enforcing a right or claim. The time period varies according to the type of claim being made. The reader is cautioned to check the applicable statutes for the appropriate jurisdiction to avoid having a claim time barred.

A statute of limitation may be tolled—that is, suspended—under certain circumstances, such as infancy of the plaintiff or absence of the defendant from the jurisdiction.

In general, when a claim is against a municipality, governmental entity or a public corporation, there is usually a requirement that the defendant be given written notice of the claim within a statutorily prescribed period of time, as a prerequisite to filing a formal lawsuit. The period of time within which the notice of claim must be filed is often quite short, e.g. 60 to 120 days.

Depending on the jurisdiction and the entity being sued, there are usually designated parties who must be served with the notice for it to be deemed sufficient. Because compliance with the statutes are mandatory—and an improperly served notice may bar a lawsuit—it is imperative that the reader check the law of the jurisdiction where the claim will be filed.

A sample Notice of Claim is set forth at Appendix 1.

CHAPTER 2:
A PERSONAL INJURY FACT PATTERN

PERSONAL INJURY FACT PATTERN

Consider this scenario:

Mary Jones is shopping in the supermarket. Unknown to her, a maintenance worker had just waxed and mopped the aisle and forgot to put up a warning sign or barrier. Mary falls on the slippery floor and injures her arm. She reports the incident immediately to the manager and leaves the store to visit her doctor, Doctor X, who has an office down the block.

As Mary exits the store, she confronts a shoplifter fleeing from a police officer. The thief pushes Mary to the ground. She hits her head and sustains a one-inch gash to her forehead. The shoplifter is apprehended and arrested. Mary declines an ambulance since she is just down the block from Doctor X's office.

Mary finally reaches Doctor X's office. She drags herself into the reception area, trying to hold her injured arm while applying a cloth to the bleeding cut on her face. She is taken into the treatment room, where she receives seven stitches to close the gash in her face. Doctor X looks at Mary's swollen and bruised arm and tells her to go home, apply a heat pack, and try and get some rest.

Mary leaves Doctor X's office. She does not have a heat pack at home, so she stops by the drugstore. Just her luck, there is a sale on the "Brand X Heating Pad System" manufactured by the Burno Company. Mary buys the product and rushes home. She takes the product out of the box and follows the instruction sheet, which reads as follows:

1. Plug in the heating pad.

2. When the blue light goes on, apply the pad to the injured area.

Mary diligently waits until the blue light goes on, at which point she applies the pad to her forearm. Unfortunately, the instructions fail to state that the user is supposed to remove the protective plastic covering on the pad before applying. As soon as Mary applies the heated pad to her forearm, the plastic covering bonds to her skin. In extreme pain, Mary calls 911 and is rushed by ambulance to the hospital, where she is treated for third degree burns to a large area of her forearm.

Mary is admitted overnight to the hospital for observation. When Mary wakes up the following morning, she is unable to move her arm, which had swelled up overnight. When Mary tells the doctor that she fell on her arm the previous day, an x-ray is ordered. The x-ray reveals that Mary suffered a broken bone in her elbow when she slipped and fell in the supermarket, and the bone had begun to set overnight in that position. The doctor must literally, and painfully, re-break Mary's bone and set it in the proper position. A cast is applied and Mary is released from the hospital.

While Mary is standing outside the hospital entry trying to hail a taxicab, she encounters her nosy neighbor, Mrs. Mouth, who asks Mary how she sustained all of her injuries. At that moment, the taxicab arrives and Mary tells Mrs. Mouth that she will have to fill her in later on the details. Mrs. Mouth gives Mary a scornful look as Mary jumps into the taxicab.

Mary is finally on her way home. One block from her house, the taxicab had to stop short to avoid hitting a dog who ran out from between two parked cars. A moment after the taxi braked for the dog, Mary heard another car screeching to a halt behind the taxi. The car couldn't stop in time and violently struck the taxi from the rear, throwing Mary around in the backseat of the taxi like a rag doll. The police arrive to the accident scene and ask Mary if she wants an ambulance. Mary does not want to return to the hospital so she painfully declines the offer, exits the taxi, and walks down the block towards her home.

As Mary nears her home, she notices that fliers are placed in the mailboxes and on all of the car windshields on her block. Curiously, Mary retrieves one of the fliers and is horrified to read the following: "Mary Jones of 123 Main Street was hospitalized for injuries she received in a bar room brawl Saturday night while in a state of extreme drunkenness." The flier wasn't signed. Mary looked around and caught a glimpse of Mrs. Mouth peering out behind her living room curtain and snickering.

Three days later, as Mary lays recuperating on the couch in front of the television, she hears the commercial spokesperson say: "Have you been injured? Call 555-5555 and speak to one of our experienced personal injury attorneys." Mary calls and makes an appointment. The next day, she meets with Ms. Lawyer and gives her a detailed account of the ordeal. Mary asks, "Do I have a case?"

Ms. Lawyer tells Mary that it appears she does have at least six potential claims for personal injury, according to the facts she presented.

CLAIM NUMBER ONE: PREMISES LIABILITY—THE SLIP AND FALL

Mary's fall in the supermarket is a classic negligence/premises liability claim known as a "slip and fall" case. The elements of a premises liability claim—and how they apply to Mary's case—are covered in Chapter 3 of this almanac. In short, the supermarket had the duty to provide a safe shopping environment for Mary and should have warned her about the dangerous condition in the aisle.

CLAIM NUMBER TWO: INTENTIONAL TORT—BATTERY

Mary's altercation with the shoplifter falls under the intentional tort of assault and battery. The elements of a battery claim—and how they apply to Mary's case—are covered in Chapter 4 of this almanac.

CLAIM NUMBER THREE: MEDICAL MALPRACTICE

Arguably, Doctor X's failure to order an x-ray of Mary's arm during her initial office visit makes him liable for the additional suffering she underwent as a result of his misdiagnosis and failure to take proper diagnostic tests. Mary's suit against Doctor X would be one for medical malpractice. The elements of a medical malpractice claim—and how they apply to Mary's case—are covered in Chapter 5 of this almanac.

CLAIM NUMBER FOUR: PRODUCT LIABILITY

The failure of the Burno Company to provide adequate instructions on the removal of the plastic covering from its product caused Mary to suffer serious burns to her arm. This claim falls under the category of product liability. The elements of a product liability claim—and how they apply to Mary's case—are covered in Chapter 6 of this almanac.

CLAIM NUMBER FIVE: AUTOMOBILE ACCIDENT

Mary's unfortunate experience as a passenger in the taxicab resulted in a minor whiplash condition. Mary's state is a no-fault liability state, which means that Mary's medical and other expenses related to the accident are covered under no-fault insurance. An overview of automobile accident law and no-fault insurance is covered in Chapter 7 of this almanac.

CLAIM NUMBER SIX: DEFAMATION

The fliers which were distributed in Mary's neighborhood contained false and defamatory allegations about Mary which caused Mary severe embarrassment and emotional distress. Mary likely has a claim for defamation, an intentional tort. The elements of a defamation claim—and how they apply to Mary's case—are covered in Chapter 8 of this almanac.

RETAINER AGREEMENT

Before Ms. Lawyer can begin to represent Mary, Mary must sign a retainer agreement with Ms. Lawyer. A retainer agreement is a contract between the lawyer and the client, which sets forth their understanding. It details the responsibilities the lawyer is agreeing to undertake and the compensation the lawyer expects to receive if there is a recovery, by verdict or settlement.

Most personal injury retainer agreements are contingency fee agreements. This means that the client does not have to pay any money up front to the lawyer in order for the lawyer to take on the case. In return, the lawyer receives a percentage of the net recovery, if there is one. If there is no recovery, the lawyer basically forgoes the legal fee. Most personal injury lawyers also advance the costs of the case, which are deducted from the gross recovery before the lawyer deducts his fee.

A sample retainer agreement in an automobile accident case is set forth at Appendix 2.

In many jurisdictions, a medical malpractice case is subject to limitations on the amount an attorney can recover for their legal fees. Therefore, the retainer agreement in a medical malpractice action may be quite different from the one used in a common negligence case.

A sample retainer agreement in a medical malpractice case is set forth at Appendix 3.

CHAPTER 3:
PREMISES LIABILITY

IN GENERAL

Premises liability is an area of personal injury law that is concerned with injuries sustained on premises which are owned or maintained by another as a result of a dangerous or unsafe condition located on that property. A premises liability claim may arise at a place of business, or in the home or on the property of another. For example, an individual may "slip and fall" on a slippery floor in the supermarket, or twist their ankle in a pothole. Liability may also attach if an individual is harmed by a third person due to a lack of security on the premises.

ELEMENTS OF A PREMISES LIABILITY CLAIM

In order to maintain a premises liability lawsuit, there must be a "responsible" party. For example, a person who trips and falls on the property of another is not automatically entitled to recover damages for his or her injuries. If an individual falls simply because he is not watching where he is going, he cannot recover no matter how severe the injuries may be, unless they are somehow connected to the negligence of another.

When a person is injured through no fault of his or her own, but due to the negligence of another, it must be determined which party is liable and subject to suit. Oftentimes, there are a number of persons or entities who may be held responsible in a premises liability case. For example, if a business rents space from the owner of the premises, both the building owner and the occupant of the space may be named as defendants. Thus, a party who is an owner or possessor of the property has a duty to use reasonable care with respect to the premises under its control, and to keep those premises in a safe condition for others. An owner or possessor may include a party which manages the premises.

Duty

The plaintiff in a premises liability action has the burden of proving that the responsible party—i.e., the owner or possessor of the property was negligent—e.g., in the maintenance of the property—and thus breached some "duty" owed to the injured person, and that this breach of duty "caused" the plaintiff's injuries. These are the basic "elements" which support the cause of action and permit the plaintiff to maintain the lawsuit.

The duty owed by the owner of possessor of the property generally depends on the status of the plaintiff, i.e., the classification of the persons on the property as either invitees, licensees, or trespassers, as further set forth below.

Invitees and licensees—those who are invited or who have permission or consent, either expressly or implied, to go on the premises of another—are owed a higher standard of care because they have permission to be on the premises. The lowest duty of care is owed to a trespasser.

Invitees

An owner is subject to liability for physical harm caused to invitees by a condition on the property if:

1. The owner knew or had reason to know of the condition and should have realized it involved an unreasonable risk of harm to invitees;

2. The owner should have expected that invitees would not have discovered or realized the dangers; and

3. The owner failed to exercise reasonable care to protect invitees from the danger.

Licensees

An owner is subject to liability for physical harm caused to licensees by a condition on the property if:

1. The owner knew or had reason to know of the condition, should have realized it involved an unreasonable risk of harm to licensees, and should have expected that licensees would not discover the danger;

2. The owner failed to exercise reasonable care to make the condition safe or to warn licensees of the condition and risk; and

3. The licensees did not know or have reason to know of the conditions and the risk involved.

Trespassers

An owner who knows, or should know, that there are trespassers who constantly intrude on the property, is liable for bodily harm caused them by an unsafe condition on the property if:

1. The condition is one the owner created or maintained;

2. The condition is likely to cause death or serious bodily harm;

3. The condition is of such a nature that the owner has reason to believe that trespassers will not discover it; and

4. The owner has failed to exercise reasonable care to warn trespassers of the condition and risk involved.

If the trespassers are children, according to the Restatement of Torts, a property owner or possessor is liable for their injuries if:

1. The place where the condition is maintained is one where the owner knows or should know that young children are likely to trespass;

2. The condition is one which the possessor knows, or should know, and which he realizes or should realize involves an unreasonable risk of death or serious bodily harm to such children;

3. The children, because of their youth, do not discover the condition or realize the risk involved in coming within the area made dangerous by it; and

4. The utility to the possessor of maintaining the condition is slight as compared to the risk to young children who trespass thereon.

Breach of Duty

Once it has been established that there is a relationship between the parties in which a duty has arisen, it must be shown that the defendant breached that duty in some manner, e.g., the owner failed to fill a deep hole in the ground which was camouflaged by brush.

Knowledge

As it pertains to licensees and invitees, a crucial element of a premises liability case is demonstrating that the property was in a "dangerous condition" when the injury occurred, and the owner or possessor had knowledge of the dangerous condition. In order to establish knowledge of the dangerous condition, the owner must have:

1. Created the condition;

2. Known the condition existed and negligently failed to alleviate the condition; or

3. The condition must have existed for such a length of time as to show that it should have been discovered and remedied.

Foreseeability and Notice

In order for the owner of possessor to be deemed negligent, there is a common law requirement that it be foreseeable that his conduct created the danger. The risk of injury to the third party must have been foreseeable for the actor to be held responsible. If a reasonable prudent person could not have foreseen the probability that injury would occur as a result of his conduct, there is no negligence and no liability.

Proximate Cause

In order to prove "causation," the plaintiff must establish that there was a direct connection between the negligence of the property owner and the injuries sustained by the plaintiff. If the plaintiff's injuries were caused by other factors, such as their own negligence, causation cannot be established. The act is a proximate cause of the injury if it was a substantial factor in bringing about the injury, and without which the result would not have occurred.

A sample premises liability complaint is set forth at Appendix 4.

For a more detailed discussion of premises liability law, the reader is advised to consult this author's legal almanac entitled Premises Liability Law, also published by Oceana Publishing Company.

PERSONAL INJURY FACT PATTERN: CLAIM NUMBER ONE

The first claim resulting from the personal injury fact pattern set forth in Chapter 2 involves a "slip and fall," a common premises liability negligence claim. If we examine the fact pattern, we find that all of the elements of negligence exist. The merchant had a duty to his customer—Mary—to keep the aisles safe. Mary would be considered an "invitee." It was certainly foreseeable that a recently mopped floor would be slippery and—absent a clear warning—that a person walking on those floors was likely to fall. The merchant breached his duty to Mary by not placing a barrier to prevent Mary from walking down that slippery aisle.

To find whether proximate cause exists, using the "but for" test, we ask: Would Mary's injury not have occurred "but for" the failure of the supermarket to place a barrier on the aisle? The answer: Yes. Using the "substantial factor" test, it is easily demonstrated that the slippery floor was a substantial factor without which Mary would not have fallen and sustained her injuries.

CHAPTER 4:
ASSAULT AND BATTERY

IN GENERAL

As discussed in Chapter 1, an intentional tort is a cause of action which requires the element of intent in addition to any other elements which must be proven to support the specific cause of action. Assault and battery is, perhaps, one of the most common of the intentional tort causes of action.

Battery is generally defined as an intentional, unprivileged, or unconsented to, harmful or offensive contact with the person of another. Tangible physical harm is not necessary for there to be a recovery for battery.

THE PRIMA FACIE CASE

In order to make out a prima facie case of battery, one must prove the elements of: (1) intent; and (2) contact.

(1) Intent

If an act is done with the intention of inflicting an offensive—but not harmful—bodily contact, or with the intention of merely causing another apprehension of either a harmful or offensive bodily contact, yet actually causing bodily contact, the actor is liable for battery even though the act was not done with the intention of bringing about the resulting harm.

Transferred Intent

If a person intentionally strikes one person, and in the process of doing so, he accidentally and unintentionally strikes a third person, there is deemed to be a transfer of the original intent and thus a battery of that third person.

(2) Contact

The actor's body does not have to actually come in contact with the plaintiff's body. Rather, all that is required for a battery to occur is the act and a resulting offensive harm.

THE DEFENSE OF PRIVILEGE

Privilege is a defense to a cause of action for battery. Thus, even if the plaintiff proves the elements of a prima facie battery case, if the defendant pleads and proves privilege, he can escape liability. As set forth below, the existence of privilege depends on special circumstances, such as whether there was consent to the act by the other party, or whether the act was necessary for the protection of some interest of the actor or the public which was so important that it justified the harm caused or threatened. Privileges include:

(1) Consent.

(2) Self-defense.

(3) Defense of others.

(4) Arrest and prevention of crime.

(5) Defense of property.

(6) Regaining land and chattels.

(7) Obeying military orders.

(8) Disciplining children.

Consent

The basic rules of consent are:

(a) One who consents cannot recover.

(b) The consent must be given by one who has the capacity to consent.

(c) Consent only applies to the act for which it is given. Once there has been termination of the consent, any additional acts are not privileged.

(d) Actions in excess of what is covered by the consent are not privileged.

Thus, if the one acted upon manifested a willingness in fact for the conduct to occur, there would be consent, and the act would be privileged. However, fraud on the part of the actor will vitiate consent, as where the victim is substantially misled concerning the nature and quality of the act intended by the actor.

In the context of sports, the players of the sport give implied consent for contact that is substantially within the rules of the game. Thus, there is deemed to be consent to contact, even if that contact causes harm, if:

(a) there was no intent to injure by the actor;

(b) the contact did not take place outside of the game; and

(c) the contact was in compliance with the rules of the game.

Self-Defense

Self-defense is a non-consensual privilege. The validity of this defense depends on both the nature of the threat and the actor's location at the time, such as in his own home.

Privilege does not exist if the actor reasonably believes that he can safely avoid the necessity of self-defense by retreating and does not do so. Nevertheless, if the actor is in his own home, he is not under the duty to retreat and privilege exists.

An actor is not privileged to use any means of self-defense intended or likely to cause bodily harm in excess of what the actor reasonably believes is necessary for his protection. Thus, the actor will be liable to the extent to which he exceeds the privilege. In such a case, the person acted upon has the right to defend himself against the actor's use of excessive force as he or she reasonably believes necessary.

For example, if Mr. Jones is confronted by an irate and threatening Mr. Smith, whose only weapon is his fists, Mr. Jones cannot pull a gun out and shoot Mr. Smith in the head. If Mr. Jones does attempt to shoot Mr. Smith, Mr. Smith is privileged to use additional force to defend himself against Mr. Jones' excessive act of self-defense.

Defense of Others

The actor's privilege of self-defense extends to defending third persons, including total strangers. The weight of authority holds that if the actor intervenes between two persons, he may use only the force that the person on whose behalf he intervenes could legally use.

One exception to this rule arises in the case of a mistake. If the actor is mistaken, even reasonably mistaken, as to the identity of the aggressor or the severity of the threat, the actor is liable if he or she uses what turns out later to have been unwarranted force.

Arrest and Prevention of Crime

Lawful arrest and conduct aimed at preventing serious crime is generally recognized as an independent source of privilege to commit what otherwise would constitute harmful battery.

Defense of Property

An actor is privileged to use reasonable force which is not intended to cause death or serious bodily harm, to defend intrusion upon his or her land, provided the following conditions exist:

(a) the intrusion is not privileged (for example, intrusion on another's property may be privileged if the intrusion is undertaken in order to save human life at the time of a catastrophe);

(b) the actor reasonably believes the intrusion can be prevented only by force; and

(c) the actor has first requested the other to leave, and the request has been disregarded, or the actor reasonably believes that the request would be useless or that substantial harm would be done before the request could be made.

Intentional infliction upon another of such force which threatens death or serious bodily harm is privileged only if the actor reasonably believes that the intruder is likely to cause death or serious bodily harm to the actor or to a third person whom the actor is privileged to protect.

Case law has held that there is no privilege to maintain a device upon one's property which would automatically inflict serious bodily harm on an intruder (e.g., a booby trap). In such a case, the owner of the property would be liable to the intruder for the harm inflicted.

Regaining Land and Chattels

Deadly force is never permitted as a means of repossessing land. Forceful repossession will only be privileged if:

(a) The other person dispossessed the actor without claim of right, or by fraud, force, or duress;

(b) The actor is entitled to immediate possession;

(c) The actor promptly acts following the dispossession;

(d) The actor asks to regain possession before using force, unless he reasonably believes such a request should be futile;

(e) The force is limited to regaining possession; and

(f) The force is reasonable.

The privilege to forcibly retake possession of chattels is similar to the above, but because chattels are more easily hidden and removed from a jurisdiction, the privilege more readily allows the actor to take emergency action in such a case.

Obeying Military Orders

Members of the armed forces are privileged to inflict harmful contacts on others if such contacts are reasonably necessary in order to comply with commands from superiors. However, this privilege only extends to lawful orders.

Disciplining Children

Parents are privileged within the bounds of reasonableness to physically discipline their children, as are others who are charged with the care of children. Parents are given wider latitude than non-parents. For example, school officials are privileged to use reasonable corporal punishment unless they are prohibited by the parent from doing so.

A sample assault and battery complaint is set forth at Appendix 5.

PERSONAL INJURY FACT PATTERN: CLAIM NUMBER TWO

The second claim resulting from the personal injury fact pattern set forth in Chapter 2 involves the intentional tort of battery. If we examine the fact pattern, we find that all of the elements of a prima facie battery claim exist. The fleeing shoplifter sees Mary witnessing his escape and, as he passes, he places his hands upon her person and pushes her to the ground. There is both intent and contact, without privilege or consent. There is also a resulting injury.

CHAPTER 5:
MEDICAL MALPRACTICE

IN GENERAL

There are three parties who have an interest in medical malpractice litigation. The two most obvious parties are the injured patient who is seeking recompense for suffering he would not have otherwise endured; and the physician or other health care provider responsible for causing the injury, who is now being sued and at risk of having a financially devastating judgment rendered against him or her.

The third party with an interest is society, which bears a financial burden as a result of the increasing medical costs and insurance premiums caused by such litigation; and experiences a less trusting and open relationship with their medical providers, who are being more and more careful and conservative in their practices so as to avoid such litigation.

THE PRIMA FACIE CASE

Negligence is the predominant theory of medical malpractice litigation. However, liability for malpractice may also result from actions which would not be considered negligence, for example, intentional misconduct, breach of contract, and invasion of privacy theories.

For the purposes of this section, the term "physician" is used in the discussion of medical malpractice actions because, as the primary medical care provider today, most medical malpractice actions involve the physician. However, it should be noted that medical malpractice is not limited to physicians but may also be committed by a number of health care professionals, including nurses, hospitals, mental health professionals, and other persons who provide medical care.

In order to recover in a medical malpractice action, the plaintiff must establish the following elements:

(1) The existence of the physician's duty to the plaintiff—that is, the physician/patient relationship;

(2) The applicable standard of care and the physician's violation of that standard;

(3) A compensable injury; and

(4) A causal connection between the physician's violation of the standard of care and the harm suffered.

The Physician/Patient Relationship

Liability for medical malpractice cannot exist unless there is a physician/patient relationship which creates a duty on the part of the physician to render acceptable medical care to the patient. The physician/patient relationship is generally found to exist where the physician undertakes to treat the patient, thus creating a professional relationship. The physician/patient relationship may also be based on a contract theory, in that the patient pays, or agrees to pay, the physician for his or her services.

Once the physician/patient relationship is deemed to have arisen, it cannot be unilaterally terminated by the physician without there being a mutual understanding by both physician and patient or the physician may be held liable for abandonment of the patient. Termination of the relationship may result when:

1. The patient terminates the relationship; or

2. The treatment undertaken is completed and further treatment is no longer necessary; or

3. The physician notifies the patient that he or she can no longer render services to the patient and either (a) refers the patient to another physician, or (b) extends a reasonable amount of time for the patient to find other suitable medical care.

The Standard of Care

The basic theory of medical malpractice involves a finding of fault on the part of the physician in that his or her conduct fell below a socially acceptable standard of medical care. Thus, without proof that the physician failed to exercise the required level of care, even when the treatment or procedure caused an injury or produced less than desirable results, the plaintiff would not win the case.

The burden of proving that the physician's medical care fell below acceptable standards rests with the plaintiff. The proof is usually necessarily demonstrated by the use of expert testimony, i.e., other physicians qualified in the particular area of medicine, who review the case and render an opinion that the defendant physician rendered negligent care.

As set forth in Section 299A of the Restatement of Torts, the standard of care is not that of the most highly skilled physician, nor is it that of the average member of the profession, but it is the standard of care that is common to those who are recognized in the profession itself as qualified and competent to engage in it.

For example, if the care rendered by the most highly skilled physician was used as the measuring stick for negligence, then the majority of physicians would automatically be found liable. Further, a physician's skill may fall below the average member of the profession, yet the physician may still be deemed qualified and competent.

Expert Testimony

The plaintiff's medical expert is called upon to testify for several purposes in the medical malpractice action:

1. To establish the applicable standard of care and demonstrate how it was violated;

2. To establish a causal connection between the negligence and the injury; and

3. To establish the extent of the injury.

The expert witness must be found competent to render his or her opinion in the matter. Thus, the expert must demonstrate that he or she is familiar with the defendant physician's specialty area; the medical procedures involved; and the applicable standard of care.

That familiarity generally results from the expert's own professional experience in the field. Where the geographic locality of the standard of care is in issue, the expert must be familiar with that setting as well. Once it is found that the expert is competent to testify, the extent of his or her experience would go to the weight given the testimony.

Expert Testimony Exceptions

In certain limited situations, expert testimony is not required. This is obviously advantageous for the plaintiff, who often finds it a difficult and costly task to obtain a physician who will testify against another member of the profession.

Defendant Physician Testimony

When the defendant physician has made statements of admission, such as that he or she made a mistake, these statements may be sufficient exceptions to the expert testimony requirement.

The Common Knowledge Exception

The exceptions to the expert testimony requirement include cases in which the negligence is comprehensible to the layperson, such as when the doctrine of "res ipsa loquitur" is invoked. Res ipsa loquitur translates into "the thing speaks for itself." Negligence may be inferred where there has been an unexplained injury of a type that does not normally occur in the absence of negligence. For example, it does not take an expert opinion to demonstrate to the jury that a surgical tool left inside a patient following surgery infers that negligence must have taken place. Further, to succeed with a res ipsa loquitur claim, the event must have been caused by an agency or instrumentality of the defendant; and must not have been due to any voluntary action or contribution by the plaintiff.

The common knowledge exception has been extended to include cases in which the fact patterns are more complex but still comprehensible to the lay person.

Informed Consent

An individual has an absolute right to prevent an unauthorized contact with his or her person. In medical malpractice litigation, treatment without the patient's consent may be actionable as battery. In addition, there are cases where the quality of the consent is challenged and the plaintiff claims lack of informed consent for the procedure. A patient gives consent to medical treatment either expressly, in writing or orally, or by implication, when he submits to a procedure.

Lack of informed consent means that the patient did not fully understand what the physician was going to do, and was injured as a result of the physician's action. Further, the patient claims that if he had known what the physician planned to do, he would not have consented and, therefore, would have avoided the injury.

Absent an emergency, if a physician is able to ascertain, in advance of an operation, all of the possible alternatives available to the physician if an unexpected situation should arise during the operation, the patient should be informed of the alternatives and given the chance to decide if those alternatives are acceptable before the physician proceeds with the operation. Once a surgeon begins an internal surgical procedure, there is a presumption of implied consent if he does other necessary procedures in the process.

A Compensable Injury

Another requirement for the plaintiff to prevail in a medical malpractice action is that the plaintiff must have sustained a compensable injury. If the plaintiff is able to establish the physician/patient relationship, and that there was a violation of the standard of care, the plaintiff still will not recover any damages if they did not sustain a compensable injury as a result of the violation.

A Causal Connection

The final requirement to establish a prima facie medical malpractice case is to demonstrate that there was a causal connection between the physician's violation of the standard of care and the harm suffered. The plaintiff will lose the case even if it is proven that there was a violation of the standard of care, if there is no causal connection established.

To determine causation, there are two common tests:

1. The "but for" test—If it can be proven that it was more probably true than not, that the patient's injury would not have occurred "but for" the defendant's actions, causation has been established under this test.

2. The "substantial factor" test—If it can be proven that the defendant physician's actions were a substantial factor in bringing about the injury, causation has been established under this test.

THE DEFENSES

In response to a medical malpractice claim, the defendant sets forth its defenses in its formal answer to the allegations contained in the plaintiff's complaint. Depending on the jurisdiction, some of those defenses are statutory, therefore, the reader is cautioned to check the law of their own jurisdictions. Some of the most common defenses to medical malpractice claims are set forth below.

Statute of Limitations

The statute of limitations may be tolled—that is, suspended—under certain circumstances, such as in situations where there has been intentional concealment or fraud on the part of the defendant, or where a foreign object is discovered in the patient's body. The statute may also be tolled when there exists a statutory disability to bringing the action, such as infancy.

The state statutes of limitations provisions are set forth at Appendix 7.

Plaintiff's Contributory Fault

The defendant may allege as a defense that the plaintiff's own actions contributed in some way to his or her injury. Depending on the jurisdiction, the plaintiff's contributory negligence may be a complete bar to recovery. Most jurisdictions, however, have enacted comparative negligence statutes as an alternative to the harshness of the recovery rules of contributory negligence. Under comparative negligence, the plaintiff's recovery may be diminished, but only according to the plaintiff's degree of culpability.

Consent or Release Forms

The defendant may set forth a defense alleging that the patient assumed the risk by either signing a consent form or a release form. However, such consent or release would not limit the health care provider's liability for negligence, even if the form purports to excuse the health care provider from acts of negligence. Such a provision would likely be unenforceable on public policy grounds.

Absence of Proximate Cause

If the plaintiff cannot prove that the act of malpractice caused the injury, the defendant will prevail. Proximate causation must be rooted in fact—the cause-in-fact—and supported by a legal connection between the action and the injury.

If there was an independent, intervening cause which breaks the causal connection between the first health care provider's negligent act and the intervening act, then the first health care provider may be excused from liability. However, if the intervening act was foreseeable, it would not be sufficient to break the causal connection.

For a more detailed discussion of medical malpractice law, the reader is advised to consult this author's legal almanac entitled The Law of Medical Malpractice, also published by Oceana Publishing Company.

PERSONAL INJURY FACT PATTERN: CLAIM NUMBER THREE

The third claim resulting from the personal injury fact pattern set forth in Chapter 2 involves medical malpractice. If we examine the fact pattern, we find that all of the elements of a prima facie claim exist. Mary visited Doctor X for treatment of her injuries, thus establishing the physician/patient relationship. It would be argued that the applicable standard of care under the circumstances would have been to order an x-ray of Mary's arm. Doctor X failed to do so. As a result, Mary sustained further unnecessary suffering. If Doctor X had ordered the x-ray, he would have properly diagnosed the broken bone and spared Mary the additional pain.

CHAPTER 6:
PRODUCT LIABILITY

IN GENERAL

In its broadest application, product liability law deals with the placement of a defective product into the hands of the consumer by the seller of the product. This means that the product is unsatisfactory in some way when it reaches the consumer. Responsibility for the defect rests with all sellers of the product who are in the distribution chain, as more fully set forth below.

Generally stated, a product should meet the ordinary expectations of the consumer. For example, the ordinary consumer does not expect to find a metal screw in a beverage can. This would indicate that there is a defect either in the manufacture or production of the product.

The injured person does not have to be the purchaser of the product in order to recover for injuries sustained, except in the minority of jurisdictions which require privity of contract to maintain a lawsuit for an action based on breach of warranty. If it was foreseeable that the person could have been injured as a result of the defect, then that person may recover damages.

A bystander who is injured as a result of a defective product has as much right to recover damages as the user of the product. In fact, the bystander is an absolutely innocent party to the occurrence, since he had no control over the purchase or use of the product, and no opportunity to make an independent judgment concerning the safety of the product.

For example, Mr. Smith purchases a gas barbecue grill which has a defective tank. The first time Mr. Smith turns on the gas, there is a tremendous explosion. A spark from the explosion catches on the clothes of Ms. Guest, who is standing approximately 10 feet from the grill, causing her to sustain second degree burns to her back. Even though Ms. Guest did not purchase the grill, and was not using the grill at the time of her injuries, it was certainly foreseeable that a person standing in the vicinity of the grill could be injured in the event of an explosion.

THE PRIMA FACIE CASE

There are three theories of liability which must be considered when bringing a product liability claim. They are (1) Negligence; (2) Breach of Warranty; and (3) Strict Liability.

Negligence

As more fully set forth in Chapter 1, to prove negligence, one must establish that there was (a) a duty; (b) a breach of that duty; (c) proximate cause; and (d) resulting damages.

Breach of Warranty

There are three types of warranties upon which a consumer relies which may be violated:

Express Warranty

An express warranty includes oral or written promises by the seller that the product will perform in a certain manner, or that the product conforms to its description.

Implied Warranty of Merchantability

An implied warranty of merchantability includes the obligation that the product is free of defects and meets the general standards of acceptability. For example, a pair of shoes should last for more than one week. If they fall apart before that time, with normal use, they are unacceptable.

Implied Warranty of Fitness for a Particular Purpose

As the name demonstrates, this warranty includes the obligation that the product meets the needs of a particular purpose. For example, a certain shoe may be advertised as reliable for mountain climbing. However, if the shoe falls apart during the activity, this would constitute a breach of warranty of fitness for the particular purpose of mountain climbing.

Strict Liability

Strict liability refers to liability in tort for harm caused by defective products without any necessity for the plaintiff to show fault on the part of the defendant.

The Defective Condition

The rule of strict liability applies only when the product is, at the time it leaves the seller's hands, in a condition not contemplated by the ultimate consumer, and which will be unreasonably dangerous to him. The seller is not liable when he delivers the product in a safe condition and subsequent mishandling or other causes make it harmful by the time it is consumed. The burden of proof that the product was in a defective condition at the time it left the seller is upon the injured plaintiff.

The injured party must prove (1) a seller; (2) a sale; (3) a defective condition; (4) an unreasonable danger to the user and all reasonably foreseeable injured parties, such as bystanders. To be unreasonably dangerous, one must show that the product was dangerous to an extent beyond that which would be contemplated by the ordinary consumer. The key to recovery in a product liability lawsuit is determining that the product was defective. Such defects may include:

Production or Manufacturing Defects

A production or manufacturing defect is proven when the product does not conform to the manufacturer's own specifications. This usually occurs randomly, such as in the scenario set forth above where the consumer found a metal screw in his beverage can.

Design Defects

Unlike a production defect, a design defect refers to a defect common to the product itself, and not occurring in a random sample. For example, a product may be designed defectively if it is found that it fails to perform safely according to ordinary consumer expectations. Further, a product may be defectively designed if there was a cost-effective alternative design which would have prevented the risk of injury.

Defective Warnings and Instructions

A product may be deemed defective if it lacks sufficient warnings or instructions. To be adequate, a warning must describe the nature and extent of the danger involved. Further, the manufacturer may be required to anticipate any foreseeable misuse of the product, and also warn of the dangers inherent in such misuse.

RESPONSIBLE PARTIES

The Manufacturer

The manufacturer of the defective product is liable pursuant to all theories of recovery. This rule applies not only to the manufacturer of the finished product, but to the manufacturer of any component of the finished product if that component was defective when it left the hands of the component manufacturer.

The Retailer

Although all sellers in the distribution chain are theoretically liable, the retailer is not involved in the manufacturing of the product. Thus, it would be difficult to find the retailer negligent in manufacturing the product. Nevertheless, if the retailer undertakes inspecting or assembling the product before it is sold, it may be found liable for failure to take reasonable care in the inspection and/or assembly of the product.

For example, a department store which sells bicycles in a boxed and unassembled state, direct from the manufacturer, would not likely be found negligent if there were a manufacturing defect in the bicycle. However, when the store offers to assemble a bicycle for a consumer as a condition of the sale, the store takes upon itself the duty to make sure that the bicycle is assembled correctly and inspected to make sure it is in safe and proper working order.

The Seller of Used Products

A person who engages in buying or selling used products is generally not susceptible to strict liability because the chain is broken. However, if the used seller does something intrusive with the product prior to sale, he may be held liable under a theory of secondary manufacture if what he did caused the defective condition.

USE OF DISCLAIMERS

A product may contain a disclaimer on its packaging which is used to deny or limit the remedies available to the injured plaintiff. There are certain requirements which must be met for a disclaimer to be considered valid. The disclaimer must be conspicuously placed on the product. A disclaimer which is located in small typeface on the inside cover of the product box would not likely be considered adequate. In addition, the language of the disclaimer must be in terms clear enough for the average consumer to understand. In addition, the disclaimer must not be unconscionable.

For example, a disclaimer cannot simply state that the manufacturer disclaims any liability if the product does not operate as advertised. This is fundamentally unfair to the consumer, who usually has no opportunity to test the product to determine whether it works and relies on the representations made by the salesperson.

A sample product liability complaint is set forth at Appendix 8.

For a more detailed discussion of product liability law, the reader is advised to consult this author's legal almanac entitled The Law of Product Liability, also published by Oceana Publishing Company.

PERSONAL INJURY FACT PATTERN: CLAIM NUMBER FOUR

The fourth claim resulting from the personal injury fact pattern set forth in Chapter 2 involves product liability. If we examine the fact pattern, we find that all of the elements of a failure to warn defect exist.

The product Mary purchased—the "Brand X Heating Pad System," manufactured by the Burno Company—contained an instruction sheet which failed to warn the consumer that the plastic covering on the heating pad was to be removed before using the product. This could be deemed a defect in the instructions and a failure to adequately warn the consumer. Because of this defect, Mary suffered injuries.

CHAPTER 7:
NO-FAULT AUTOMOBILE LEGISLATION

IN GENERAL

Prior to the enactment of no-fault insurance legislation, recovery for personal injuries sustained as a result of an automobile accident was subject to common law negligence rules—the "tort liability" system. Under this tort-based system, an accident victim recovers damages for both economic and non-economic damages from the party who was responsible for causing the accident (the "third party"), and recovers under the bodily injury protection coverage of that party's insurance policy. Such damages include property damage, medical expenses, lost wages and general damages, e.g., pain and suffering.

Problems with the tort-based system prompted a need for insurance reform. For example, as in any personal injury case, the accident victim must prove the responsible party's negligence in order to prevail—a time consuming process. Contributory and comparative negligence rules also apply which, depending on the jurisdiction, may limit or prevent the plaintiff's recovery. Further, the liability limits of the wrongdoer's liability insurance, if in fact there is insurance, may be so low that it does not fully compensate the accident victim for his or her losses.

NO-FAULT AUTOMOBILE INSURANCE

Under no-fault, the accident victim recovers benefits for such losses as medical expenses and lost wages from his or her own insurer in a first party claim, rather than suing the negligent party in a third party claim for such compensation. Nevertheless, problems still exist in the implementation of the various no-fault schemes, largely because they still permit tort recovery if the accident victim meets certain criteria—known as the "serious injury" threshold. If so, the injured party may bring a lawsuit for damages against the negligent driver. The complaint must allege that the plaintiff's injuries exceed the no-fault serious injury threshold.

Under a pure no-fault system, accident victims would receive substantial benefits to compensate them for their losses. However, they would have no legal right to pursue a lawsuit against the party responsible for the accident.

THE NEW YORK STATE NO-FAULT INSURANCE SYSTEM

As discussed below, New York has enacted typical no-fault legislation that covers personal injuries sustained in motor vehicle accidents in New York State. While the New York law provides a basic overview of a typical no-fault system, the reader is advised to check the law of his or her own jurisdiction when filing a claim.

Following a motor vehicle accident, it is important that an injured person notify the appropriate insurance carrier to claim their no-fault benefits. If the claim for no-fault benefits is not made within the statutory time period, which is presently 90 days, the no-fault benefits will likely be denied.

If a person is injured on a bus or a school bus in New York State, the law requires that no-fault benefits must be paid under that person's automobile insurance policy or under the policy of a relative with whom that person resides if he or she does not have an automobile. If no person in the household has automobile insurance, the no-fault claim may then be made to the insurance carrier for the bus company.

Once the no-fault claim is made, a no-fault claim number and claims representative will be assigned to the case. The name and address of the insurance carrier, the name and telephone number of the claims representative, and the claim number should be provided to all health care providers. In addition, out-of-pocket expenses, including pharmacy receipts and mileage claims should be sent directly to the no-fault claims representative.

No-Fault Benefits

The New York no-fault law provides for the payment of benefits to victims of motor vehicle accidents to reimburse them for their "basic economic loss." A person is entitled to no-fault benefits regardless of who was at fault for the accident. Briefly summarized, basic economic loss consists of up to $50,000 per person in benefits for the following:

1. All necessary doctor and hospital bills and other health service expenses, payable in accordance with fee schedules established or adopted by the New York State Insurance Department.

2. Eighty (80%) percent of lost earnings up to a maximum monthly amount of $2,000 for up to three years following the date of the accident.

3. Up to $25 per day for a period of one year from the date of the accident for other reasonable and necessary expenses the injured person may have incurred because of an injury resulting from the accident, such as the cost of hiring a housekeeper or necessary transportation expenses to and from a health service provider.

No-fault benefits also include a $2,000 death benefit, payable to the estate of a covered person, in addition to the $50,000 coverage for basic economic loss outlined above. Once the initial coverage has been exhausted, additional benefits may be available if the applicable insurance policy has been endorsed to include Optional Basic Economic Loss coverage and/or Additional Personal Injury Protection coverage.

The no-fault benefits outlined above continue to be paid until it is medically determined that the injured person is no longer in need of services. We recommend that the client keep a daily journal of all medical appointments, expenses, and other relevant information. At some point during the period following the accident, the claims representative will set up an appointment with its own health care provider to conduct an "independent medical examination." Based upon the medical report, the claims representative will either continue or deny all or part of the benefits. The injured person may contest any denials to the State Insurance Department or resort to the arbitration process to try and have the no-fault benefits reinstated.

Recovery for Pain and Suffering: Meeting the No-Fault Threshold

Following the accident, a claim for pain and suffering due to bodily injury is generally made to the insurance carrier which represents the person responsible for the accident. Once the bodily injury claim is made, a bodily injury claim number and claims representative is assigned to this part of the claim, which is separate and distinct from the no-fault claim. This may or may not be the same insurance carrier as the no-fault carrier, depending on the circumstances and parties involved.

Under New York State's no-fault insurance law, in order to recover monetary compensation for "pain and suffering" as a result of the personal injuries sustained in a motor vehicle accident, a claimant's injuries must satisfy the "serious injury" requirement. This standard is known as the "no-fault threshold."

Under the law, a "serious injury" is defined as "a personal injury which results in:

(1) death;

(2) dismemberment;

(3) significant disfigurement;

(4) a fracture;

(5) loss of a fetus;

(6) permanent loss of use of a body organ or member;

(7) significant limitation of use of a body organ or member;

(8) significant limitation of use of a body function or system; or

(9) a medically determined injury or impairment of a non-permanent nature which prevents the plaintiff from performing substantially all of the material acts which constitute plaintiff's usual and customary daily activities for not less than ninety days during the one hundred-eighty days immediately following the occurrence of the injury or impairment."

It is customary for the no-fault insurance carrier to require the injured claimant to submit to an "independent" medical examination during the course of their treatment. Oftentimes, particularly when the claimant's injuries are soft tissue injuries, the results of the medical examination will favor the carrier, and state that the claimant no longer requires medical or other no-fault benefits. Based on this information, the insurance carrier generally denies all or a portion of the no-fault benefits. If the claimant disagrees with this determination, they are entitled to submit the dispute to arbitration, or they may bring a lawsuit to require the insurance carrier to pay no-fault benefits.

A sample complaint to recover no-fault benefits is set forth at Appendix 9.

Evaluating the Case for Litigation Purposes

Once the client has substantially completed his or her medical treatment, a review and evaluation of the medical records is undertaken to determine whether the client has met the criteria outlined above. An evaluation is also made of settlements and verdicts for similar injuries under similar circumstances. Based on this review and evaluation, a document is generally prepared and sent to the claims representative detailing the claimant's injuries and an assessment of liability and potential exposure. It is after this point that settlement negotiations with the insurance carrier proceed.

If there is no liability, or the medical records clearly indicate that the client has not met the no-fault threshold, the insurance carrier will most likely deny any monetary settlement. If the medical records indicate that it is questionable whether the client has sustained injuries that meet the no-fault threshold, the insurance carrier may also deny settling the case, although most will negotiate in good faith and offer some type of settlement if there is some doubt as to whether or not the no-fault threshold has been met. In offering a settlement under this scenario, the insurance carrier will generally consider such factors as the cost of retaining a lawyer to defend the case and the likelihood that they will be able to have the case dismissed early on in the lawsuit.

Bodily injury claims are scrutinized very carefully by insurance carriers to determine whether the no-fault threshold has been reached. If an insurance carrier denies settling a case, or makes what appears to be an insignificant offer of settlement, the only recourse is to file a lawsuit. However, in cases where it is clear that the client will not meet the no-fault threshold, a lawsuit may not be recommended. Insurance carriers who do not believe a case has satisfied the "significant injury" requirement will make a motion to the court to dismiss the case for failure to meet the no-fault threshold. These motions are commonly granted in cases where serious injury is difficult to prove and unsupported by medical records.

In addition, the court, in its discretion, may award costs and attorney's fees to the defendant or their attorney if it finds that the plaintiff or plaintiff's attorney engaged in frivolous conduct. In addition, the court can also impose financial sanctions against the plaintiff or plaintiff's attorney for pursuing a frivolous action.

Of course, if the medical records indicate that the client has suffered serious injuries which are compensable under the law, it is likely that the insurance carrier will act in good faith in settling the claim. However, if they do not settle the matter within a reasonable period of time, a lawsuit may be commenced to recover monetary damages for the client's pain and suffering as a result of the accident, provided the plaintiff can establish a prima facie negligence case against the defendant.

The statute of limitations, the period within which the lawsuit must be filed, is generally 3 years from the date of accident. However, a shorter statute of limitations may apply if a governmental entity or municipality is involved as a party. The reader is advised to check the applicable statute of limitations in his or her jurisdiction.

A sample complaint in a automobile accident case which occurs in a no-fault jurisdiction is set forth at Appendix 10.

During the course of litigation, it is possible that the case will settle at any time up to and including trial. The time period between filing the lawsuit and the trial can be very lengthy due to congested court calendars and the litigation process itself. If the case does not settle during this period, a verdict will be rendered by the jury for either the defendant or the plaintiff. If the plaintiff prevails, damages will be awarded in a monetary sum as determined by the jury according to the evidence presented during trial.

For a more detailed discussion of no-fault insurance law, the reader is advised to consult this author's legal almanac entitled The Law of No-Fault Insurance, also published by Oceana Publishing Company.

PERSONAL INJURY FACT PATTERN: CLAIM NUMBER FIVE

The fifth claim resulting from the personal injury fact pattern set forth in Chapter 2 involves automobile accident liability, a common negligence claim. Mary' s state is a no-fault state. As set forth above, she is entitled to recover for all of her economic losses. It is questionable whether Mary's whiplash condition can meet the "serious injury" threshold. However, if Mary's incapacitation is prolonged, it is possible that she can seek a monetary recovery for pain and suffering under the "catch-all" category which defines a serious injury as one which incapacitates the person for at least 90 out of the 180 days following the accident.

CHAPTER 8:
DEFAMATION

IN GENERAL

Defamation is an intentional tort cause of action which has its roots in the biblical admonition: "Thou shalt not bear false witness against thy neighbor." The Restatement (Second) of the Law of Torts defines a defamatory communication as one which "tends so to harm the reputation of another as to lower him in the estimation of the community, or to deter third persons from associating or dealing with him."

See §559 of the Restatement (Second) of the Law of Torts. Note that all provisions of the Restatement (Second) of the Law of Torts cited in this chapter are set forth at Appendix 11.

The concept of communication involves the bringing of an idea to the perception or knowledge of another person. It is not necessary that the defamatory communication lower the person in the eyes of everyone in the community. A substantial minority will satisfy the statute.

If the defamatory communication is made about a deceased person, the speaker is not liable either to the estate of the deceased, or to his or her family members.

See §560 of the Restatement (Second) of the Law of Torts.

Nevertheless, the survival statutes of a particular jurisdiction govern whether an action for defamation survives the defamed person's death. Readers are advised to check the statutes of their jurisdictions on this issue.

Libel and Slander Distinguished

There are two components which make up the law of defamation: libel and slander. Libel refers to written or visual defamation, and slander refers to oral or spoken defamation. Libel and slander are further distinguished in the Restatement (Second) of the Law of Torts, as follows:

(1) Libel consists of the publication of defamatory matter by written or printed words, by its embodiment in physical form or by any other form of communication that has the potentially harmful qualities character- istic of written or printed words.

(2) Slander consists of the publication of defamatory matter by spoken words, transitory gestures or by any form of communication other than those stated in Subsection (1).

(3) The area of dissemination, the deliberate and premeditated charac- ter of its publication and the persistence of the defamation are factors to be considered in determining whether a publication is a libel rather than a slander.

See §568 of the Restatement (Second) of the Law of Torts.

Slander

Where the slanderous communication is not actionable per se, as dis- cussed below, it is nonetheless actionable if it is the legal cause of special harm to another. Thus, the plaintiff in a slander case is generally required to prove that he or she suffered special damages, i.e., actual pecuniary in- jury, as a result of the slanderous communication.

See §575 of the Restatement (Second) of the Law of Torts.

The plaintiff is entitled to recover damages for the special harm that was caused by the slanderous communication, as well as damages for general loss of reputation, and for any resulting emotional distress, illness or other bodily harm.

Slander Per Se

According to the Restatement (Second) of the Law of Torts, an exemption to the special damages requirement for slander claims exists if the defam- atory statement imputes one of the below-listed conditions or behaviors to the plaintiff.

Criminal Conduct

A showing of special damages is not required if the slanderous remark im- putes to another conduct constituting a criminal offense. The offense, however, must be one which would be punishable by imprisonment in a state or federal institution, or a crime which is regarded by public opinion as involving moral turpitude.

Moral turpitude is generally defined as behavior which is so extreme a departure from ordinary standards of honesty, good morals, justice, or ethics, that it shocks the moral sense of the community.

See §571 of the Restatement (Second) of the Law of Torts.

Loathsome Disease

A showing of special damages is not required if the slanderous remark imputes to another an existing venereal disease, or other loathsome and communicable disease. To be actionable per se, however, the statement must indicate a present infection with the disease.

See §572 of the Restatement (Second) of the Law of Torts.

Business/Trade/Profession/Office

A showing of special damages is not required if the slanderous remark imputes to another conduct or other characteristics which would adversely affect that person's fitness for his or her lawful business, trade, profession, or public/private office. This rule is applicable not only to the individual, but also protects corporations and their agents or officers.

See §573 of the Restatement (Second) of the Law of Torts.

Sexual Misconduct

A showing of special damages is not required if the slanderous remark imputes to another serious sexual misconduct. This rule does not require criminal conduct, but applies to charges such as unchastity, adultery, and fornication.

See §574 of the Restatement (Second) of the Law of Torts.

If the defamatory statement imputes one of the foregoing behaviors or conditions to the plaintiff, the defamatory statement is known as slander per se and does not require a showing of special harm.

See §570 of the Restatement (Second) of the Law of Torts.

Libel

It is generally easier to maintain a cause of action for libel. This is because libel, being in a written form, is likely to cause a more permanent injury to the plaintiff's reputation; is easily spread to a larger audience; and more readily demonstrates the defendant's intent in making the defamatory statement.

Libel Per Se

The Restatement (Second) of the Law of Torts provides that a communication which is deemed libelous is also libelous per se, i.e., it does not require any proof of special damages. This was the rule at common law, but only a minority of jurisdictions adhere to this rule today.

See §569 of the Restatement (Second) of the Law of Torts.

Some jurisdictions will only consider a defamatory statement libel per se if the defamatory meaning is readily apparent. If extrinsic facts must be introduced to explain the libelous nature of the defamatory statement, the plaintiff will be required to prove special damages to maintain the action, as in common slander claims. Nevertheless, many jurisdictions further provide that if the statement is one which falls into any of the four slander per se categories, proof of special damages is not required.

ELEMENTS OF A DEFAMATION CAUSE OF ACTION

The Restatement (Second) of the Law of Torts, sets forth the elements necessary to maintain a defamation cause of action, as follows:

False Statement

At common law, the falseness of a defamatory statement was assumed and the burden was on the defendant to prove that the statement was true as his or her defense. This rule still constitutionally applies in cases where the plaintiff is a private figure or the subject matter is of no public interest. The requisite standard is generally proof by a preponderance of the evidence.

When the plaintiff is a public official, or a public figure, it is the plaintiff who has the burden of proving that the defamatory statement is false. Further, the plaintiff may be required to prove falsity "with convincing clarity," the overriding concern being the constitutional protection of truth telling.

The U.S. Supreme Court has yet to rule on whether the burden of proof shifts to the plaintiff to prove falsity in cases where the plaintiff is a private person, and the subject matter is of public interest.

Regardless of who has the burden of proof on the truth or falsity of the statement, if the statement is substantially true, it is generally not actionable, and presents a complete defense to a defamation case. This rule applies provided any false statements or minor inaccuracies do not present significantly greater injury to the plaintiff's reputation than does the full recitation of the facts.

Defamatory Nature of the Statement

In general, a statement may be defamatory in nature if it injures one's reputation. This is usually accomplished through the use of words, although that is not always the case. The extent to which a statement may be deemed to have injured one's reputation varies among the jurisdictions, and bears on whether the statement will be considered defamatory. Thus, readers are advised to check the law of their own jurisdictions.

A statement which is unflattering, vulgar, embarrassing, or merely hurts one's feelings, may be displeasing to the plaintiff, but is generally not actionable. If such actions were permitted, the courts would likely be inundated with defamation claims.

The key distinction is whether or not the statement will actually injure the plaintiff's reputation. The Restatement (Second) of the Law of Torts defines a defamatory statement as one that is so injurious to the plaintiff's reputation that it will "lower him in the estimation of the community" or will "deter third persons from associating or dealing with him."

Actual Malice

Where the plaintiff is a public official or public figure, libel by implication must be accompanied by actual malice by the defendant for there to be liability. The constitutional standard of actual malice requires knowledge of the falsity of the statement or reckless disregard for the truth, by the defendant.

DEFENSES

The primary defenses to a claim for defamation include (i) truth; (ii) privilege; (iii) consent; (iv) sovereign immunity; and (v) opinion, as further set forth below.

Truth

At common law, truth was considered an absolute defense to a claim of defamation. Truth is still generally available as a defense in cases involving private plaintiffs concerning matters of no public interest.

See §581A of the Restatement Second of the Law of Torts.

Although the doctrine that truth is generally unactionable still holds true, constitutional considerations in cases involving public plaintiffs, or issues of public concern, have shifted the burden of proof to the plaintiff, who must demonstrate the falsity of the statement.

Further, some jurisdictions have enacted constitutional or statutory provisions which bar truth as a defense if the statement is: (1) published for malicious motives; (2) if there is no justifiable purpose for publishing the statement; or (3) if the statement concerns matters of public interest.

Privilege

At common law, there are two types of privileges which enable an individual to make defamatory statements. They are (1) absolute privilege; and (2) conditional privilege—also known as "qualified privilege."

Absolute Privilege

The existence of absolute privilege depends on the speaker's position or status. If the speaker is entitled to absolute privilege, he or she is given total immunity from liability for defamatory statements. Absolute privilege extends to certain public officials in the course of performing their official duties, as set forth below.

The rationale for granting this absolute privilege is the notion that individuals in certain positions require complete freedom of speech so that their duties may be properly carried out. If an individual is deemed to be entitled to absolute privilege, personal motives cannot thereafter be imputed if the defamatory statement is made while the individual is acting in his or her official capacity. Therefore, evidence of recklessness or malice is irrelevant and will not defeat the immunity.

Positions for which absolute privilege applies include:

1. Judicial Officers

2. Attorneys At Law

3. Parties To and Witnesses in Judicial Proceedings

4. Jurors

5. Participants in Judicial Proceedings

6. Federal Officials

7. Congress

8. Witnesses in Legislative Proceedings

9. State Officials

10. State Legislators

11. State Agencies and Administrators

12. Spouse

13. Publication Required by Law

Conditional Privilege

Conditional privilege is not concerned with the role of the speaker, but focuses on the circumstances under which the defamatory statement was made.

At common law, the defendant was permitted to plead and prove that he or she had either a duty to make the defamatory statement, or a legitimate interest to protect by making it. To obtain this privilege, however, the speaker must act in good faith, without malice, and without abusing the privilege.

The rationale underlying this privilege is that, under certain circumstances, the good that may be accomplished by permitting someone to make a defamatory statement without fear of liability outweighs the harm that may be done to the reputation of others.

An example of conditional privilege is the generally recognized right of credit reporting agencies to gather information concerning an individual, and provide this information to a subscriber for the purpose of extending credit to the individual.

These credit reports may contain negative information, which may be false or outdated, concerning the credit profile of the individual. However, absent a showing of recklessness, bad faith, or malicious intent, the privilege will likely be upheld.

The Restatement (Second) of the Law of Torts sets forth six circumstances in which a person has a conditional or qualified privilege to make defamatory statements:

1. Protection of the Speaker's Own Interests

2. Protection of Recipient or Third Party Interests

3. Protection of Interests in Common

4. Protection of Interests Among Family Members

5. Protection of Public Interests

6. Communications by Inferior Public Officials

See the Restatement (Second) of the Law of Torts.

Abuse of Privilege

There are certain circumstances which will defeat the privilege to make defamatory statements with immunity, as set forth below.

Common-Law Malice

A showing of malice towards the plaintiff will defeat a claim of conditional privilege if the plaintiff can show that the defamatory statement was unrelated to the privilege claimed, and that there existed a predominant improper motivation on the part of the speaker, including spite, ill will, hatred or the intention to inflict harm.

Actual Malice

Actual malice is the constitutional standard of malice concerned with the defendant's disregard for truth, rather than his or her ill will towards the plaintiff. Actual malice has been defined as publication of a defamatory statement with knowledge of its falsity or subjective awareness of its probable falsity. Actual malice has been deemed evidence of common-law malice in order to defeat conditional privilege because the Courts have reasoned that there is no valid reason to protect the interests of a liar.

See §600 of the Restatement Second of the Law of Torts.

Recklessness

Recklessly false statements have been held to be conclusive evidence of common-law malice for the purpose of defeating conditional privilege because it demonstrates ill will on the part of the speaker.

Negligence

Negligence is defined as a lack of reasonable grounds for belief in the truth of a defamatory statement. Courts are divided as to whether negligence on the part of the speaker should defeat the conditional privilege.

Excessive Publication

Excessive publication of a defamatory statement to a person who is not the proper recipient of such communication abuses the privilege.

See §604 of the Restatement Second of the Law of Torts.

Consent

Consent to the publication of a defamatory statement by the person who has been defamed, is a complete defense to any cause of action for defamation by that person. However, the nature of the consent must be examined to determine the scope of the consent given. This rule applies even if the person does not know that the statements to which he or she is consenting are, or will be, defamatory. It is sufficient if he or she is aware of the exact language of the publication, or that it may be defamatory.

It has been held that conduct which gives apparent consent sufficiently bars recovery. Further, if the person to whom the consent is given reasonably interprets the conduct as consent to the publication of the defamatory matter for all purposes, the publication would likely be privileged. However, if the consent is limited to publication to a particular individual, or for a particular purpose or time, those limitations must be adhered to for the privilege to attach.

See §583 of the Restatement Second of the Law of Torts.

Sovereign Immunity

The federal government has absolute sovereign immunity against all tort claims, unless specifically waived by statute. The federal government has not waived its immunity from defamation claims. State governments also have sovereign immunity from tort claims unless specifically waived by statute. The reader is cautioned to check the law of their own jurisdictions when contemplating a defamation claim against a particular state.

Opinion

At common law, the privilege of "fair comment" was a defense to a defamation claim. This doctrine was inspired by the same concern for freedom of expression and free debate which motivated the constitutionalization of defamation law by the U.S. Supreme Court.

The "fair comment" doctrine was deemed inadequate due to the uncertainty of its application, which could deter the freedom of expression it purported to protect. A speaker was still subject to a judge or jury's interpretation of whether his or her comments were fair or unfair, opinion or fact.

The U.S. Supreme Court sought to correct this uncertainty through a series of cases in which the court rejected the notion that the correctness of an opinion be ruled upon by a judge or jury, and further stated that: "Under the First Amendment, there is no such thing as a false idea." The majority of courts have ruled that opinion is constitutionally protected speech and not actionable.

THE BURDEN OF PROOF

The burden of proof refers to the requirement of the party to persuade the jury to find in his or her favor on an issue, and to introduce sufficient evidence to support and justify that finding.

See § 613 of the Restatement (Second) of the Law of Torts.

Plaintiff's Burden

In an action for defamation, the plaintiff has the burden of proving the following issues when they are properly raised in the case:

1. The defamatory character of the communication;

2. Publication of the communication by the defendant;

3. Application of the communication to the plaintiff;

4. The recipient's understanding of the defamatory meaning of the statement;

5. The recipient's understanding that the statement was intended to apply to the plaintiff;

6. Special harm resulting to the plaintiff from publication of the statement;

7. The defendant's negligence, reckless disregard or knowledge regarding the truth or falsity and defamatory character of the communication; and

8. The defendant's abuse of a conditional privilege.

Defendant's Burden

In an action for defamation, the defendant has the burden of proving, when the issue is properly raised, the presence of the circumstances necessary for the existence of a privilege to publish the defamatory communication.

Further, in certain cases involving private individuals, the defendant may still retain the burden of proving the truth of the defamatory statement. In cases which involve public officials/public figures, this burden has been shifted to the plaintiff to prove the defendant's negligence or greater fault regarding the falsity of the statement. However, this issue is not yet settled by the U.S. Supreme Court in cases involving private plaintiffs.

A sample defamation complaint is set forth at Appendix 12.

It is important to note that a cause of action for defamation has a shorter statute of limitation than a negligence claim. Thus, the complaint must be filed prior to the date the statute of limitations expires.

A table of state statutes of limitations for defamation claims is set forth at Appendix 13.

For a more detailed discussion of defamation law, the reader is advised to consult this author's legal almanac entitled The Law of Libel and Slander, also published by Oceana Publishing Company.

PERSONAL INJURY FACT PATTERN: CLAIM NUMBER SIX

The sixth claim resulting from the personal injury fact pattern set forth in Chapter 2 involves defamation, a common intentional tort claim. If we examine the fact pattern, we find that all of the elements of a prima facie libel claim exist. Mary's neighbor "published" written false information defaming Mary's character to third parties—Mary's neighbors.

CHAPTER 9:
LIABILITY AND DAMAGES

LIABILITY

Once it has been established that there is indeed liability for the injuries sustained by the plaintiff, the extent of that liability, and its apportionment, must be determined. This chapter discusses the various forms liability takes, and how the plaintiff's own actions impact the liability of the defendants.

Joint and Several Liability

Joint and several liability may be imposed when multiple parties are responsible for the plaintiff's injury. A distinction may be drawn between the actions of the defendants, as follows:

(1) Concerted Action—All defendants are responsible for the harm actually caused by only one. For example, if two cars are racing and one car accidently strikes the plaintiff, both cars are equally liable to the plaintiff for the harm suffered.

(2) Independent Action—All defendants are responsible when defendants act independently, each causing harm to the plaintiff, but the degree cannot be allocated among them. For example, plaintiff is a passenger in Car A, which collides with Car B due to the fault of both drivers. A and B are thus jointly and severally liable to the plaintiff for the harm suffered.

Case law has held that when two defendants are both negligent, but only one of them could have caused the plaintiff's injury, the court will hold both of them liable if it cannot determine which of the defendants caused the damage. In such a case, it is the defendants who must come forward with evidence to absolve themselves. This shifts the burden of proof to the defendants. Otherwise, the plaintiff would never be able to prove who actually caused the injury.

Another example involves an unexplained injury which occurs during a medical procedure to a part of the body not under treatment. The doctrine of res ipsa loquitur ("the thing speaks for itself") applies against all of the doctors and medical employees who take part in caring for the patient. If the plaintiff were required to prove who was responsible for the injury, it is possible that the medical personnel would keep silent to avoid implicating a colleague and the injured plaintiff would never recover.

Contributory Fault

Contributory fault refers to those situations in which the plaintiff's own actions contribute in some way to their harm.

Assumption of Risk

Assumption of risk refers to the common-law doctrine which states that a plaintiff may not recover for an injury when he has voluntarily exposed himself to a known danger. For example, a spectator at a sporting event who sits in an open area assumes the risk of being hit by a ball.

Contributory Negligence

Contributory negligence refers to conduct on the part of the plaintiff which falls below the standard to which he should conform for his own protection, and which is a legally contributing cause cooperating with the negligence of the defendant in bringing the plaintiff harm. The burden of proving the plaintiff's contributory fault is on the defense. If contributory negligence is found, under the common law, the plaintiff was barred from recovery. There are exceptions, as set forth below:

Last Clear Chance Doctrine—The Helpless Plaintiff

The plaintiff may recover if he negligently subjects himself to harm caused by the defendant's negligence if, immediately preceding the harm:

(1) the plaintiff is unable to avoid the harm by exercise of reasonable care; or

(2) the defendant fails to use reasonable care to avoid the harm when the defendant:

(a) knows plaintiff's situation and realizes the peril involved, or

(b) would discover the situation and have reason to realize the peril if he were to exercise the vigilance which is his duty to exercise.

Last Clear Chance Doctrine—The Inattentive Plaintiff

The plaintiff may recover if, by exercise of reasonable vigilance, he or she could have discovered the danger created by the defendant's negligence in time to avoid the harm, only if the defendant:

(1) knows of the plaintiff's situation;

(2) realizes or has reason to realize the plaintiff is inattentive and unlikely to discover the peril in time to avoid the harm; and

(3) is thereafter negligent in failing to utilize with reasonable care and competence his existing opportunity to avoid causing harm to the plaintiff.

Comparative Negligence

Comparative negligence refers to a statute change introduced in many jurisdictions to counteract the harshness of the recovery rules of contributory negligence and assumption of risk. Under comparative negligence rules, recovery may be diminished, but only according to the plaintiff's degree of culpability.

Vicarious Liability

When third persons are held liable for the conduct of others, they are said to be vicariously liable. We assume both the identity of the actor and the wrongful nature of his conduct, and ask whether liability may be extended beyond the actor to include persons who have not committed a wrong or directly caused any harm, but on whose behalf the wrongdoing actor acted.

The concept of vicarious liability is one of considerable practical importance to the plaintiff because it is an effective means of providing a financially responsible defendant. For example, in certain situations, employers may be held liable for the torts of their employees. This principle is derived from the common law master/servant relationship and is known as the doctrine of "respondeat superior." This doctrine, as well as other forms of vicarious liability relationships, are explained below.

Respondeat Superior

The most important principle establishing vicarious liability for the tortious conduct of another is the doctrine of respondeat superior: A master is vicariously liable for the torts of his servants committed while the latter are acting within the scope of their employment.

The "servant" need not be performing precisely the activity for which he was hired in order to expose the master to liability, and the tortious conduct need not involve physical injury. Thus, the officers of our major corporations are considered "servants" in the legal sense of the word. Also, the "servant" need not be receiving a wage, but may be performing services out of a sense of friendship for another.

In contrast to "servants," independent contractors are persons hired to do jobs under circumstances which, as a general rule, do not call for the application of the doctrine of respondeat superior.

If the tortfeasor is an independent contractor, the general rule is that the employer is not vicariously liable for the harm caused by the contractor's wrongful conduct.

Joint Enterprise

When two or more persons join together in an enterprise in which each has an equal right to control the other's conduct, one might apply master-servant concepts upon each participant in relation to the other participant. For example, in a partnership, each partner is generally liable for the acts of the other partners.

Family Purpose Doctrine

This doctrine is a special judicially developed rule which, under certain circumstances, imposes liability upon the owner of a family automobile for harm negligently caused to others by a family member while operating the automobile for a family purpose with permission.

Successor Corporation Liability

When Corporation A and Corporation B conduct a formal merger and become Corporation C, C is liable for the torts that A and B may have committed prior to the merger.

Liability of a Minor for Tortious Acts

Various state statutes make parents liable for the willful and malicious conduct of minors. The age of seven is generally thought to be the age when a child should be able to understand his conduct. A minor who is a party to litigation is represented by a guardian ad litem, who acts on the minor's behalf.

There is a generally accepted rule that minors who engage in adult activities are to be judged by an adult standard. Most courts ignore distinctions based upon whether the issue is the minor's primary negligence or contributory negligence.

Death of an Injured Party Prior to Judgment

One may be under the impression that if the injured party dies before there is a recovery, the defendant is "off the hook." However, by statute, the death of the injured party prior to judgment has far less devastating effects upon existing or potential rights to recover against a tortious defendant. Two types of statutes accomplish this result:

Survival Statutes

Survival Statutes prevent abatement of existing causes of action due to the death of either party. The basic measure of recovery is what the decedent would have been able to recover for the injuries if he had survived.

Wrongful Death Statutes

Wrongful death statutes create causes of action that allow recovery when the tortious conduct of the defendant causes someone to die. The basic measure of recovery is the harm caused to the decedent's family by the defendant's conduct.

A table of state wrongful death statutes is set forth at Appendix 14.

DAMAGES

Once it has been determined that there is liability, the question turns to whether damages were caused as a result of the wrongful conduct. In personal injury law, damages are usually measured in terms of monetary compensation. There are three categories of money damages recoverable in a personal injury case: (1) compensatory damages; (2) punitive damages, and (3) nominal damages.

Compensatory Damages

Compensatory damages represent an attempt to compensate the injured party for the actual harm he suffered, by awarding the amount of money necessary to restore the plaintiff to his pre-injury condition. Often, a complete restoration cannot be accomplished. In such cases, damages also include the monetary value of the difference between the plaintiff's pre-injury and post-injury conditions. Typical items include those listed below.

Medical Expenses

Medical expenses are the most concrete and objectively demonstrable items to identify. The expense must be reasonably related to the defendant's wrongful conduct.

Lost Earnings and Impairment of Earning Capacity

Lost earnings and impairment of earning capacity are the most justifiable element of a general compensatory damages award from a strictly economic point of view. Recovery is sought for:

(1) the earnings actually lost up to the time of the trial or settlement; and

(2) the diminution in the plaintiff's capacity to earn in the future.

Pain, Suffering, and Other Intangible Elements

Pain and suffering is the most difficult element of recovery to measure. This is a broad concept, which may include a number of more or less separate factors, the most common of which is the physical pain associated with the injury. Recovery for mental suffering associated with bodily disfigurement is also includible as an element of pain and suffering.

Another element is the loss of enjoyment in relation to life in either all of its aspects, or merely certain aspects. For example, if a plaintiff enjoyed playing piano as a hobby, and has suffered an injury to his hands, the plaintiff has suffered a loss of enjoyment in relation to the ability to play the piano. Of course, if this were the plaintiff's livelihood, the damages for loss of earning capacity would also be involved, and would greatly increase the measure of damages.

Injury to Personal Property

The rules in case of injury to personal property are simple and straightforward. The basic measure is the difference between the market value of the property before the injury and its market value after. If the property has been totally destroyed, the market value after the injury will be the salvage value, if any. The cost of repairs are included, in addition to payment for devaluation, if any, after repair. The plaintiff may also be able to recover for the loss of use of the property while it is repaired or replaced, as long as it is within a reasonable time period.

Punitive Damages

Punitive damages involve an award of a substantial amount of money to the plaintiff for the purpose of punishing the defendant. Thus, punitive damages are usually only awarded if the defendant acted with malice or reckless indifference to the plaintiff.

Liability insurance is the usual source of recovery for personal injury claims. However, in cases involving intentional torts, such as battery, insurance generally does not cover the wrongdoer. In the absence of insurance coverage, claims must be paid out of the defendant's personal assets.

Nominal Damages

A nominal damages award involves a very small amount of money, awarded merely for the purpose of showing that the plaintiff was legally wronged.

CHAPTER 10:
FINAL RESOLUTION

As set forth below, a personal injury claim may be resolved by going through a trial and obtaining a verdict; by means of alternative dispute resolution; and by negotiation and settlement.

LITIGATION AND VERDICT

Litigation is the most formal, and the most time-consuming of the dispute resolution methods. Litigation is complicated, costly, and can go on for years. The parties to the litigation are each responsible for developing their own legal theory, and providing their evidence, in order to prove their case and prevail in the dispute. The judge or jury considers all of the evidence and arguments set forth by the parties. Once the parties have set forth their case, the judge or jury is entrusted to make the final decision.

The final resolution of litigation occurs when the finder of fact—the judge or jury—renders a verdict for either the plaintiff or the defense. In a bifurcated trial, the issue of liability is resolved first and, if liability is determined, a second trial is held to determine the extent of the damages suffered by the plaintiff, and the apportionment of the liability. If there is a defense verdict, the case is dismissed and the plaintiff loses. Of course, the plaintiff always has the option of appealing the decision if there are adequate grounds to support an appeal.

ALTERNATIVE DISPUTE RESOLUTION

Alternative dispute resolution (ADR) refers to the practice of resolving a disagreement to the satisfaction of all parties, in an expedient and economically feasible manner, rather than litigating the dispute. Another advantage of alternative dispute resolution is that it affords the parties complete confidentiality, unlike court records which are open to the public.

There are various methods of alternative dispute resolution, with differing degrees of formality. The primary methods of alternative dispute resolution include (i) arbitration and (ii) mediation.

Arbitration

Arbitration is the process whereby an impartial third party, known as an arbitrator, listens to both sides of the dispute and issues a binding decision.

The Uniform Arbitration Act is set forth at Appendix 15.

Mediation

Mediation is a less formal method of alternative dispute resolution than arbitration. Mediation, like arbitration, enlists the assistance of a neutral third party, known as a mediator. However, the role of the mediator differs from that of the arbitrator. The mediator does not issue a binding decision but rather assists the opposing parties in resolving their own dispute, which resolution may then be formalized in a written agreement.

A national directory of organizations offering dispute resolution services is set forth at Appendix 16.

The American Arbitration Association

The American Arbitration Association is a not-for-profit public service organization which maintains a roster of nearly 17,000 impartial experts—known as neutrals—who hear and resolve cases. The neutrals are recognized for their standing and expertise in their fields, and their integrity and dispute resolution skills. The conduct of arbitrators is guided by the AAA's Code of Ethics, prepared by a Joint Committee of the American Arbitration Association and the American Bar Association. The conduct of mediators is governed by the Model Standards of Conduct for Mediators, developed by the American Arbitration Association, the American Bar Association and the Society of Professionals in Dispute Resolution.

A national directory of American Arbitration Association (AAA) offices is set forth at Appendix 17.

For a more detailed discussion of alternative dispute resolution, the reader is advised to consult this author's legal almanac entitled The Law of Alternative Dispute Resolution, also published by Oceana Publishing Company.

NEGOTIATION AND SETTLEMENT

Negotiation is the least formal method of resolving a dispute without litigation. For negotiation to succeed, the participants must be able to openly and patiently communicate with each other, even though they may disagree. Negotiation follows no established rules or guidelines. It is entirely voluntary and conducted between the parties to the negotiation, or their representatives. There are no third party intermediaries available to assist the negotiators in reaching a settlement.

Negotiation presents a scenario of offers and counter-offers concerning resolution of a particular dispute, until the parties reach that magic middle ground on which they can mutually agree—the settlement. A settlement may be judicial or non-judicial. A non-judicial settlement is one which is reached between the parties without court intervention. A judicial settlement is one which is reached during the pendency of a lawsuit, usually with the supervision and guidance of the trial judge. In general, the policy of all courts is to encourage settlement and discourage litigation.

Once an agreement has been reached, a final written document encompassing all of the negotiated points should be drafted and signed by the parties. Depending on the nature of the dispute, a settlement agreement may also include a release of claims. By signing a release, a party gives up all right to pursue the claims stated in the release. This is both the motivation and consideration for entering into the settlement agreement.

A sample general release of claims is set forth at Appendix 18.

TYPES OF SETTLEMENTS

The primary types of settlement agreements include the following:

Lump Sum Settlement

The lump sum settlement is the most common type of settlement, which generally requires the payment of a sum of money in exchange for the release of the other party's claims.

Sliding-Scale Settlement

A sliding scale settlement includes a condition in which it is agreed that an adjustment may be made to the settling defendant's obligation dependent upon any amounts which may ultimately be recovered from the nonsettling defendants.

Structured Settlement

The structure settlement allows for the payment of money, in installments, over a period of time. The structured settlement is usually used when the recovery is significant and the paying party is financially unable to make a lump sum payment, or in cases involving minors. Generally, the plaintiff receives payments from a trust or annuity which is funded by the defendant.

APPENDIX 1:
SAMPLE NOTICE OF CLAIM

In the Matter of the Claim of

JOHN DOE, Claimant   NOTICE OF CLAIM

     -against-

THE NEW YORK CITY DEPARTMENT OF
TRANSPORTATION AND THE CITY OF
NEW YORK, Respondents

TO: THE NEW YORK CITY DEPARTMENT OF TRANSPORTATION
       THE CITY OF NEW YORK

SIRS:

PLEASE TAKE NOTICE that the claimant herein hereby makes a claim and demand against the City of New York, as follows:

    1. The name and post-office address of claimant and his attorney is:

        Claimant: John Doe
                 79-11 41st Avenue
                 Elmhurst, New York 11373

        Attorney: [Attorney Name]
                 [Attorney Address and Telephone Number]

    2. The nature of the claim is: Personal injuries sustained by claimant as a result of a fall caused by a large, deep and uneven depression located on a public street.

    3. The time, place and manner in which the claim arose: The incident complained of took place on October 19, 1999 at approximately 12:00 p.m. in the afternoon, on 43rd Avenue at the intersection of Bell Boulevard in the County of Queens, City of New York. Claimant was crossing the street in the crosswalk when he stepped immediately to the left of

---

the crosswalk to avoid a turning vehicle. Claimant stepped into the aforementioned depression and fell to the ground. Claimant was taken from the scene by ambulance to the hospital.

4. The items of damage claimed are: The Claimant sustained ankle injuries, including a severe ankle sprain and contusions, and has otherwise suffered bodily pain and suffering and emotional distress. Claimant is presently undergoing evaluation and treatment for said injuries thus, the extent of the damages are not presently knowable. Said claim and demand is hereby presented for adjustment and payment.

5. This notice is made and served on behalf of said infant in compliance with the provisions of Section 50-e of the General Municipal Law and such other laws and statutes as are in the case made and provided.

WHEREFORE, I respectfully request that this claim be allowed and paid by the said NYC Department of Transportation and The City of New York.

Dated: South Salem, NY
         November 15, 1999

_____
[Attorney Name/Address/Tel. No.]

TO: *Via Certified Mail*

         Office of the City Comptroller
         Bureau of Law and Adjustment
         1 Centre Street, room 1220
         New York, New York 10007

APPENDIX 2:
SAMPLE RETAINER AGREEMENT IN AN AUTOMOBILE ACCIDENT CASE

RETAINER AGREEMENT

DATED this 15th day of July, 2000, the undersigned, JOHN DOE ("Client"), retains and employs [name of attorney] ("Attorney") as his attorney to represent him with full authorization to do all things necessary to investigate and settle any and all negligence claims arising from an automobile accident which occurred on June 15, 2000, and to initiate legal action if in Attorney's judgment such action is warranted after a full investigation has been made.

The undersigned agrees to the following terms and conditions:

1. Attorney has agreed to take client's case on a contingency fee basis. This means that attorney's legal fees will be paid only if client receives a monetary judgment or settlement in this matter. Attorney will receive no fee if there is no recovery.

2. The contingency fee in this matter will be one-third (1/3) of any amount recovered by settlement or judgment. In addition, it may be necessary for Attorney to advance certain expenses during the course of litigation. Such expenses, if any, shall be subtracted from any sum recovered after the attorney fee is deducted. If no recovery is made, Client will not be responsible for any attorney fee whatsoever.

3. Client understands and agrees that Attorney cannot commence work in this matter until this agreement is signed and returned to attorney's office.

4. Attorney agrees not to enter into any settlement agreement without the consent of Client.

5. Attorney acknowledges that a payment in the amount of $_____ accompanies this retainer agreement.

6. By signing below where indicated, Client acknowledges that he has received a copy of this retainer letter and has read and agreed to its terms and conditions.

ACCEPTED BY: _____

John Doe, Client

The above employment is hereby accepted on the terms stated.

ACCEPTED BY: _____

[Attorney Signature Line]

APPENDIX 3:
SAMPLE RETAINER AGREEMENT IN A
MEDICAL MALPRACTICE CASE

RETAINER AGREEMENT

DATED this 24th day of April, 2000, the undersigned, JANE DOE ("Client"), 79-11 41st Avenue, Elmhurst, New York 11373, retains and employs [name of attorney] ("Attorney") as her attorney to represent her with full authorization to do all things necessary to prosecute or adjust a claim for damages arising from personal injuries sustained by Client arising out of the negligent diagnosis of a tissue specimen by XYZ Laboratories.

The undersigned agrees to the following terms and conditions:

1. Client hereby gives Attorney the exclusive right to take all legal steps to enforce this claim through trial and appeal. The attorney shall have the right but not the obligation to represent Client on appeal.

2. Attorney has agreed to take Client's case on a contingency fee basis. This means that attorney's legal fees will be paid only if Client receives a monetary judgment or settlement in this matter. Attorney will receive no fee if there is no recovery.

3. In consideration of the services rendered and to be rendered, Client agrees to pay Attorney and authorizes Attorney to retain out of any recovery by judgment or settlement in this matter, the following fees applicable to medical malpractice claims under the law:

    (a) 30 percent on the first $250,000 of the sum recovered,

    (b) 25 percent on the next $250,000 of the sum recovered,

    (c) 20 percent on the next $500,000 of the sum recovered,

    (d) 15 percent on the next $500,000 of the sum recovered,

(e) 10 percent on any amount over $1,250,000 of the sum recovered,

(f) one-third on sums recovered on account of non-medical malpractice claims, such as simple negligence and breach of contract claims, if any.

4. Such percentage shall be computed on the net sum recovered after deducting from the amount recovered expenses and disbursements for expert testimony and investigative or other services properly chargeable to the enforcement of the claim or prosecution of the action. In computing the fee, the costs as taxed, shall be deemed part of the amount recovered. For the following or similar items there shall be no deduction in computing such percentages: liens, assignments or claims in favor of hospitals, for medical care and treatment by doctors and nurses, or self-insurers or insurance carriers.

5. In the event extraordinary services are required, Attorney may apply to the court for greater compensation pursuant to the Special Rules of the Appellate Division regulating the conduct of attorneys.

6. In addition, it may be necessary for Attorney to advance certain out-of-pocket expenses during the course of litigation. Client agrees to reimburse Attorney for her pro-rata share of expenses advanced on her behalf. Such expenses, to the extent that they have not been prepaid, shall be subtracted from any sum recovered after the attorney fee is deducted. In the event no recovery is made, Client is still responsible for payment of expenses. Attorney acknowledges that a retainer in the amount of $ _____ has been received by Client to be applied against actual out-of-pocket expenses, as they accrue. A statement of expenses shall be sent to Client on a regular basis.

7. If the cause of action is settled by Client without the consent of Attorney, Client agrees to pay Attorney the above percentage of the full amount of the settlement for the benefit of Client, to whomever paid. The Attorney shall have, in the alternative, the option of seeking compensation on a quantum meruit basis to be determined by the court. In such circumstances, the court would determine the fair value of the service. Attorney shall have, in addition, Attorney's taxable costs and disbursements. In the event Client is represented on appeal by another attorney, Attorney shall have the option of seeking compensation on a quantum meruit basis to be determined by the court.

8. If Attorney is terminated by Client prior to resolution of this matter, Client agrees to pay all legal fees and costs incurred for services rendered on Client's behalf thus far, at Attorney's hourly rate, which is cur-

rently $_____ per hour, unless both Attorney and Client agrees, in writing, to other payment arrangements prior to such termination.

9. If it becomes necessary to engage the services of any outside experts, such as accountants, psychologists, medical professionals or other expert witnesses, Clients will be notified in advance. If Client agrees that the services of any such experts are required, Client will retain their services and agree to be responsible for the costs of such services. In the event that Attorney advances the expert's fees on Client's behalf, such advanced fees are considered an expense of litigation as set forth in Paragraph 6.

10. This agreement does not concern any appellate litigation resulting from this matter. If appellate litigation becomes necessary, a new retainer agreement will be required prior to Attorney representing Client in such litigation.

11. Client understands and agrees that Attorney cannot commence work in this matter until this agreement is signed and returned to Attorney's office. By signing below where indicated, Client acknowledges that she has received a copy of this retainer letter and has read and agreed to its terms and conditions.

ACCEPTED BY: _____

Jane Doe, Client

The above employment is hereby accepted on the terms stated.

ACCEPTED BY: _____

[Attorney Signature Line]

APPENDIX 4:
SAMPLE PREMISES LIABILITY COMPLAINT

[NAME OF COURT]

[CAPTION OF CASE] [FILE INDEX NUMBER]

COMPLAINT

Plaintiff, by his attorney, [name of attorney], complaining of the defendant, alleges, as follows:

FIRST: Plaintiff is a resident of the City, County and State of New York.

SECOND: Upon information and belief at all times hereinafter mentioned the defendant was and still is a domestic corporation, duly organized and existing under and by virtue of the laws of the State of New York.

THIRD: Upon information and belief at all times hereinafter mentioned the defendant owned a supermarket located at 1 Main Street, New York, New York 10001, in the Borough of Manhattan, City and State of New York.

FOURTH: Upon information and belief, at all times hereinafter mentioned the defendant managed, operated, maintained and controlled those premises.

FIFTH: That the public, and more particularly, the plaintiff, were invited to the premises of the defendant for the purpose of purchasing various grocery items from the defendant.

SIXTH: That on the 27th day of March, 2000, the plaintiff, while lawfully on the above premises, was caused to fall, due to the negligence of the defendant, its agents, servants and/or employees.

SEVENTH: That the defendant, its agents, servants and/or employees were negligent in that they failed to clean a slippery substance from the floor of an aisle in the premises and failed to warn the public, and more particularly, the plaintiff, of the dangerous condition existing on the premises, and in generally being careless and reckless concerning the hazardous condition on the premises.

EIGHTH: Upon information and belief at that time and place defendant had actual knowledge and notice of the dangerous condition existing on the premises or the condition had existed for a sufficient length of time prior to the accident such that the defendant could and should have had such knowledge and notice.

NINTH: That the accident and resulting injuries were due to the negligence of the defendant, its agents, servants and/or employees.

TENTH: That as a result of the negligence of the defendant the plaintiff was rendered sick, sore, lame and disabled and suffered serious and painful injuries in and about his head, body and limbs, and has been informed and believes that he will continue to suffer therefrom for an indefinite period of time in the future and that such injuries may be permanent in nature.

ELEVENTH: That by the reason of the negligence of the defendant, the plaintiff has been damaged in the sum of One Hundred Thousand ($100,000) Dollars.

WHEREFORE, plaintiff demands judgment against defendant in the amount of One Hundred Thousand ($100,000) Dollars; costs and disbursements of this action; and any other relief the Court deems appropriate.

PLEASE TAKE NOTICE, that pursuant to the CPLR, you are required to serve a copy of your answer within 20 days after the service of this Complaint.

Dated:

[Signature Line]

      [Name of Attorney]

      Attorney for Plaintiff

      [Attorney's Address]

      [Attorney's Telephone Number]

APPENDIX 5:
SAMPLE ASSAULT AND BATTERY
COMPLAINT

[NAME OF COURT]

[CAPTION OF CASE] [FILE INDEX NUMBER]

COMPLAINT

Plaintiff, by his attorney, [name of attorney], complaining of the defendant, alleges, as follows:

FIRST: Plaintiff is a resident of the City, County and State of New York.

SECOND: Upon information and belief at all times hereinafter mentioned the defendant was and still is a resident of the City, County and State of New York.

THIRD: On or about the 12th day of January, 2000, at approximately 10:00 o'clock in the forenoon of that day, the plaintiff was lawfully and properly waiting for a public bus on the bus stop designated for that purpose located at the intersection of Kissena Boulevard and Jewel Avenue, in the County of Queens, City of New York, State of New York.

FOURTH: At that time, date and location, defendant approached plaintiff and, without provocation, willfully, wantonly, maliciously and recklessly assaulted and beat plaintiff and struck plaintiff in the head, face and neck with a metal object, causing plaintiff to sustain the injuries hereinafter alleged.

FIFTH: Solely by reason of the foregoing, plaintiff became sick, sore, lame, and disabled and remains so, and suffered and still suffers great physical and mental pain, and sustained severe injuries to the head, face and neck, and other injuries, and was obliged to expend large sums of money for medical treatment, and has been informed and believes his injuries are permanent.

SIXTH: By reason of the foregoing, the plaintiff has been damaged in the sum of Two Hundred Fifty ($250,000) Dollars.

WHEREFORE, plaintiff demands judgment against defendant in the amount of Two Hundred Fifty ($250,000) Dollars; costs and disbursements of this action; and any other relief the Court deems appropriate.

PLEASE TAKE NOTICE, that pursuant to the CPLR, you are required to serve a copy of your answer within 20 days after the service of this Complaint.

Dated:

[Signature Line]

      [Name of Attorney]

      Attorney for Plaintiff

      [Attorney's Address]

      [Attorney's Telephone Number]

APPENDIX 6:
SAMPLE MEDICAL MALPRACTICE
COMPLAINT FOR WRONGFUL DEATH AND
NEGLIGENCE AGAINST HOSPITAL

[CAPTION OF CASE]

Plaintiff, by his attorney, complaining of the defendant, alleges upon information and belief as follows:

AS AND FOR A FIRST CAUSE OF ACTION—NEGLIGENCE

1. On the 1st day of June, 1999, the plaintiff, JOHN SMITH (hereinafter referred to as "John Smith" or "administrator"), was duly appointed administrator of the estate of his father, PETER SMITH, deceased, upon the issuance of Limited Letters of Administration by the Surrogate's Court of the County of Nassau, State of New York.

2. Plaintiff, JOHN SMITH, at all times hereinafter mentioned resided at [insert plaintiff's address].

3. Plaintiff's decedent, PETER SMITH (hereinafter referred to as "Mr. Smith," "Father" or "decedent" or "plaintiff"), at all times hereinafter mentioned resided, at [insert decedent's address]

4. Upon information and belief, at all times hereinafter mentioned, the Defendant ANYTOWN CITY HOSPITAL (hereinafter referred to as "Anytown" or "hospital"), was and still is a domestic corporation duly organized and existing under and by virtue of the laws of the State of New York, which operates and maintains a hospital facility, with its principal place of business located at [insert hospital address].

5. Upon information and belief, Defendant ANYTOWN, its agents, servants, and/or employees managed, maintained, operated and were in con-

trol of said hospital, which holds itself out as a hospital duly qualified and capable of rendering adequate medical care and treatment to the public, and for such purposes employs doctors, nurses, and other personnel.

6. Upon information and belief, the Defendant ANYTOWN, and its employees, undertook the medical care and treatment of the Plaintiff's decedent, PETER SMITH on January 1, 1998

7. Upon information and belief, the Defendant, ANYTOWN, and its employees, rendered medical treatment to PETER SMITH during the time period of January 1, 1998 until his death on January 5, 1998.

8. The Plaintiff was at all time using due care.

9. The medical care, diagnosis, assessment and treatment rendered by Defendant ANYTOWN and its employees was performed in a negligent and careless manner, as more fully set forth herein and in the following statement of facts, and constitutes professional negligence and malpractice resulting in severe, conscious physical and mental pain and suffering of Plaintiff's decedent, PETER SMITH, prior to death, resulting in his wrongful death on January 15, 1998.

10. The Defendant, ANYTOWN, was careless in its employment and supervision of doctors, nurses, and other medical personnel and employees, causing severe, physical and mental personal injuries and conscious pain and suffering to Plaintiff's decedent resulting in his death on January 5, 1998.

11. Plaintiff alleges the doctrine of respondeat superior.

STATEMENT OF FACTS

12. On January 1, 1998, plaintiff's decedent fell in their home and was taken by ambulance to Anytown City Hospital complaining of neck, back and shoulder pain.

13. The decedent arrived at the emergency room of defendant ANYTOWN at approximately 11:30 p. m. On January 1st, immobilized in a neck brace, and brought to the emergency room.

14. Decedent's family was advised by decedent's employee, an emergency room resident, that after such a fall as the one taken by the decedent, there was always the possibility of a spinal fracture. The family was further advised that a CAT scan of decedent's neck and head would be ordered and performed.

15. Thereafter, the defendant failed to perform the aforementioned CAT scan and/or x-ray of decedent's neck and head. On January 5, 1998, the defendant proceeded to discharge the decedent.

16. On the day of discharge, the plaintiff arrived at the hospital to assist the decedent in preparing for discharge.

17. Decedent was not wearing a neck stabilizing brace nor had he had any x-rays or cat scans of his neck despite constant pain.

18. When decedent attempted to get out of the bed, his chin fell to his neck and he lost all feeling in his arms and legs.

19. Plaintiff summoned a nurse to the scene, who assisted plaintiff in returning the decedent to the bed.

20. Plaintiff requested that a neck brace be placed on the decedent and that a CAT scan be taken.

21. Nevertheless, the defendant did not order a CAT scan and did not stabilize plaintiff's neck.

22. Later that same evening, plaintiff received a telephone call from the hospital advising him that the decedent's neck had broken and he had been rendered quadriplegic and would die within several days.

23. On January 5, 1998, decedent died.

24. Defendant, ANYTOWN, its servants and/or employees, were careless and negligent in failing to timely perform a neck CAT scan on their patient, Peter Smith.

25. Defendant, ANYTOWN, its servants and/or employees, were careless and negligent in failing to stabilize the patient's neck.

26. Defendant, ANYTOWN, its servants and/or employees, were careless and negligent in failing to carefully examine the patient;

27. Defendant, ANYTOWN, its servants and/or employees, were careless and negligent in failing to properly diagnose the patient's condition.

28. Defendant, ANYTOWN, its servants and/or employees, were careless and negligent in failing to administer adequate treatment to the patient.

29. Defendant, ANYTOWN, its servants and/or employees, were careless and negligent in failing to properly monitor the patient;

30. Defendant, ANYTOWN, its servants and/or employees, were careless and negligent in failing to recognize spinal injury;

31. Defendant, ANYTOWN, its servants and/or employees, were careless and negligent in failing to adequately treat spinal injury;

32. Defendant, ANYTOWN, its servants and/or employees, were careless and negligent in failing to properly heed the complaints of the patient.

33. Defendant, ANYTOWN, its servants and/or employees, were careless and negligent in failing to comply with the patient and his family's request for a neck brace.

34. Defendant, ANYTOWN, its servants and/or employees, were careless and negligent in failing to comply with the patient and his family's request for a neck CAT scan.

35. Defendant, ANYTOWN, its servants and/or employees, were careless and negligent in failing to carefully handle and otherwise attend to the patient's needs;

36. Defendant, ANYTOWN, its servants and/or employees, were careless and negligent in failing to act with sufficient urgency;

37. By reason of the foregoing, Plaintiff's decedent has been damaged in the sum which exceeds the jurisdiction of any other court which has jurisdiction over this matter.

38. This action falls within the exceptions to CPLR 1602.

AS AND FOR A SECOND CAUSE OF ACTION—GROSS NEGLIGENCE

39. Plaintiff repeats and realleges each and every allegation contained in Paragraphs "1" through "38" of this Complaint, inclusive, as though fully set forth herein.

40. In the medical care, diagnosis, assessment, and treatment rendered by Defendant ANYTOWN CITY HOSPITAL, its servants and/or employees, to the Plaintiff's decedent PETER SMITH, Defendant was sufficiently careless, reckless, wanton and/or malicious so as to constitute gross negligence.

41. In its employment and supervision of doctors, nurses, and other medical personnel, Defendant ANYTOWN CITY HOSPITAL was sufficiently careless, reckless, wanton and/or malicious so as to constitute gross negligence.

42. By reason of the foregoing, the Plaintiff's decedent, PETER SMITH, has been damaged in the sum which exceeds the jurisdiction of any other court which has jurisdiction over this matter.

43. Based on the aforementioned, Plaintiffs are entitled to punitive damages.

AS AND FOR A THIRD CAUSE OF ACTION

44. Plaintiffs repeat and reallege each and every allegation contained in Paragraphs "1" through "43" of this Complaint, inclusive, as though fully set forth herein.

45. Defendant ANYTOWN, its servants and/or employees, prior to the granting or renewing of privileges or employment of Defendant's servants and/or employees, including interns, residents, nurses, doctors and others involved in the Plaintiff's decedent's care, failed to investigate the qualifications, competence, capacity, abilities and capabilities of said servants and/or employees, including but not limited to obtaining the following information: patient grievances, negative health care outcomes, incidents injurious to patients, medical malpractice actions commenced against said persons, including the outcome thereof, any history of association, privilege and/or practice at other institutions, and discontinuation of said association, employment, privilege and/or practice at said institutions, and any pending professional misconduct proceedings in this State or another State, the substance of the allegations in such proceedings and any additional information concerning such proceedings and the findings of the proceedings; and further failed to make sufficient inquiry of the physician, nurse and/or employees and institutions which should and did have information relevant to the capacity, capability, ability and competence of said persons rendering treatment.

46. Had the Defendant made the above-stated inquiry or in the alternative had it reviewed and analyzed the information obtained in a proper manner, privileges and/or employment would not have been granted and/or renewed.

47. By reason of the Defendant ANYTOWN'S failure to meet the aforementioned obligation, plaintiff's decedent was were treated by physicians, nurses and/or other employees who were lacking the requisite skills, abilities, competence and capacity, as a result of which plaintiff's decedent was injured and died.

48. By reason of the foregoing, the Plaintiffs have been damaged in the sum which exceeds the jurisdiction of any other court which has jurisdiction over this matter.

CERTIFICATE OF MERIT

A certificate of merit is annexed hereto.

JURY DEMAND

Plaintiffs demand a jury trial on all issues triable by jury.

RELIEF REQUESTED

WHEREFORE, Plaintiff demands judgment against Defendant ANYTOWN CITY HOSPITAL for each cause of action in an amount as the jury may justly award in accordance with CPLR 3017(c), together with the costs and disbursements of this action.

Dated: Anytown, New York
        July 1, 1999
        Yours, etc.
        [Attorney Name and Address]

VERIFICATION

STATE OF NEW YORK)

      : ss.

COUNTY OF NASSAU)

JOHN SMITH, residing at 100 Main Street, Anytown, New York 11530, having been duly sworn, deposes and says that he is a Administrator of the Estate of PETER SMITH, the deceased plaintiff in the above entitled action; that he has read the foregoing Complaint and knows the contents thereof; that the same are true of his own knowledge, except as to matters therein stated to be alleged upon information and belief, and as to those matters he believes it to be true.

[DATE AND TOWN]

      ATTORNEY SIGNATURE LINE

      ATTORNEY NAME/ADDRESS/TELEPHONE

[NOTARY STAMP]

APPENDIX 7:
STATE STATUTES OF LIMITATIONS IN MEDICAL MALPRACTICE CASES

JURISDICTION	STATUTE	APPLICABLE PROVISION
Alabama	Code of Alabama, §6-5-482	Within 2 years from date of injury unless injury not discovered or reasonably discoverable then suit must be brought within 6 months after discovery or when reasonably discoverable; no suit may be brought more than 4 years after date of injury; minors under 4 years must bring suit by 8th birthday if statute would have otherwise expired by that time.
Alaska	Alaska Statutes, §09.10.070	Within 2 years from date claimant discovers, or reasonably should have discovered, the existence of all elements essential to the cause of action; tolled by disability.
Arizona	Arizona Revised Statutes, § 12-542	Within 2 years from date of injury, tolled by disability.
Arkansas	Arkansas Statutes Annotated, §16-114-203	Within 2 years from date of accrual of cause of action; accrual of cause of action shall be date of wrongful act complained of and no other time; if latent condition due to foreign object then 1 year from discovery or reasonable discover- ability; a minor aged 9 or younger with a claim as a result of obstetrical care shall have until 2 years after ninth birthday; adjudicated incompetent must bring suit within 1 year of removal of disability.

JURISDICTION	STATUTE	APPLICABLE PROVISION
California	California Civil Procedure Code, §340.5	Within 3 years from date of injury or 1 year after discovery or reasonable discoverability, whichever occurs first; in no event more than 3 years after injury unless fraud, concealment, or a foreign object; minor under 6 must bring suit within 3 years or before 8th birthday, whichever is longer.
Colorado	Colorado Revised Statutes, § 13-80-102.5	Within 2 years from date of accrual but in no event more than 3 years from act; if concealment or foreign object then 2 years from discovery; if minor under 8 and less than 6 at time of injury must bring claim by age of 8.
Connecticut	Connecticut General Statutes Annotated, §52-584	Within 2 years from injury or discovery of injury or reasonable discoverability but not more than 3 years after act or omission.
Delaware	Delaware Code Annotated, Title 18, §6856	Within 2 years from injury or 3 years from date of injury if not discoverable; minor is same as adult or must sue by 6th birthday.
District of Columbia	DCS §12-301; 302	Within 3 years from accrual of cause of action for negligence; 1 year for battery; disability tolls statute.
Florida	Florida Statutes Annotated, § 95.11	Within 2 years from act, discovery of act, or reasonable discovery of act, but not more than 4 years; if fraud, concealment of injury or intentional misrepresentation prevented discovery within 4 year period, suit must be brought within 2 years from discovery or reasonable discovery, but in no event may suit be brought more than 7 years after act.
Georgia	Georgia Code, §9-3-71-73	Within 2 years from injury or death but in no event longer than 5 years from act or death; 1 year after discovery if foreign object; minor under 5 years shall have 2 years from date of 5th birthday to bring action but in no event later than 10th birthday or 5 years from date of negligence; legally incompetent person must file no more than 5 years after date in which negligence, wrongful act, or omission occurred.

JURISDICTION	STATUTE	APPLICABLE PROVISION
Hawaii	Hawaii Revised Statutes, Title 32, §657-7.3	Within 2 years from discovery or reasonable discoverability but in no event more than 6 years after act; statute is tolled during any period where the person has failed to disclose any act, error or omission upon which the action is based and which is known or reasonably knowable by that person; minors must bring action within 6 years of act or 10th birthday, whichever is longer.
Idaho	Idaho Code, §5-219	Within 2 years from act; if foreign object or fraudulent concealment then 1 year from discovery or reasonable discovery or 2 years from act, whichever is later.
Illinois	735 ILCS 5/13-212	Within 2 years from discovery or reasonable discovery of injury but in no event more than 4 years from act; statute is tolled during period plaintiff is insane, mentally ill, or imprisoned; minors must bring suit within 8 years after act but in no event after age 22.
Indiana	Indiana Code Annotated, § 16-9.5-3-1	Within 2 years from act; minor under 6 years shall have until 8th birthday to file suit; statute applies regardless of minority or other disability.
Iowa	Code of Iowa, §614.1	Within 2 years from discovery or reasonable discoverability but in no event longer than 6 years after act unless foreign object left in body.
Kansas	Kansas Statutes, §60-513	Within 2 years from act or reasonable discoverability but in no event more than 4 years after act.
Kentucky	Kentucky Revised Statutes, § 413.140	Within 1 year from discovery or reasonable discoverability but in no event more than 5 years after act.
Louisiana	Louisiana Revised Statutes Annotated, §9:5628	Within 1 year from act or date of discovery but in no event more than 3 years from date of act regardless of minority or disability.
Maine	Maine Revised Statutes Annotated, Title 24, §2902	Within 3 years after act; minors must bring action within 6 years after accrual of cause of action or within 3 years of majority, whichever occurs first.

JURISDICTION	STATUTE	APPLICABLE PROVISION
Maryland	Maryland Courts & Judicial Procedure Code Annotated, § 5-109	Within 5 years from act or 3 years from discovery, whichever is shorter; for minors statute begins to run at age 11; exceptions to statute if damages affect reproductive system or caused by foreign object.
Massachusetts	Massachusetts General Laws Annotated, Chapter 260, §4; Chapter 231, §60D	Within 3 years after cause of action accrues but in no event more than 7 years after act or omission unless foreign object; minors must bring action within 3 years from accrual of cause of action but if under 6 years of age statute does not begin to run until 9th birthday but in no event more than 7 years from act or omission unless foreign object.
Michigan	Michigan Comp. Laws, § 27a.5805, 5851, 5856	Within 2 years from act or 6 months from discovery or reasonable discovery; disabled plaintiff has 1 year from removal of disability except minors under 13 years have until 15th birthday; 6 years from date of injury except for reproductive injury, foreign object or fraudulent concealment.
Minnesota	Minnesota Statutes, §541.07	Within 2 years from act.
Mississippi	Mississippi Code Annotated, § 15-1-36	Within 2 years after discovery or reasonable discoverability; minor or mentally incompetent plaintiff has within 2 years after disability ends but minor age 6 or under at time cause of action accrues has 2 years from time of 6th birthday or death, whichever occurs first.
Missouri	Missouri Revised Statutes, § 516.105	Within 2 years from act unless foreign object which is 2 years from discovery or reasonable discoverability but in no event longer than 10 years from act; minors under 10 must bring suit by 12th birthday.
Montana	Montana Code Annotated, § 27-2-205	Within 3 years from act or discovery or reasonable discover- ability, whichever occurs first but in no event more than 5 years from act; statute is tolled for failure of disclosure of act; minors must file within 3 years of 8th birthday or death, whichever occurs first.
Nebraska	Revised Statutes of Nebraska § 44-2828	Within 2 years from act or 1 year from discovery but not more than 10 years after date of service which is basis for suit.

JURISDICTION	STATUTE	APPLICABLE PROVISION
Nevada	Nevada Revised Statutes, § 41A.097	Within 4 years after injury or 2 years after discovery or reasonable discovery, whichever occurs first; for minors statute is tolled until age 10 for brain damage or birth defects; if sterility alleged statute runs 2 years after discovery.
New Hampshire	New Hampshire Revised Statutes Annotated, §508:4, 508:8	Within 3 years from act or omission or discovery or reasonable discovery; minor or incompetent must bring suit within 2 years of removal of disability.
New Jersey	New Jersey Revised Statutes, §2A:14-2	Within 2 years after accrual of claim.
New Mexico	New Mexico Statutes Annotated, §41-5-13	Within 3 years from date of malpractice regardless of minority or disability except minors under 6 have until 9th birthday to file suit; statute is tolled upon submission to hearing panel and shall not run until 30 days after panel's final decision.
New York	New York Civil Practice Laws and Rules, §214-a	Within 2-1/2 years from act or last treatment where there is continuous treatment for condition giving rise to claim; if foreign object 1 year from discovery or reasonable discovery.
North Carolina	North Carolina General Statutes, §1-15	Cause of action shall arise at time of occurrence of last act giving rise to cause of action; where damages not readily apparent and damage is discovered or reasonably discovered 2 or more years after occurrence of last act of defendant, suit must be commenced within 1 year from date discovery is made; nothing herein shall reduce the statute to less than 3 years but in no event more than 4 years from last act; if foreign object within 1 year from discovery but in no event more than 10 years from last act.
North Dakota	North Dakota Cent. Code, § 28-01-18; 25	Within 2 years from discovery but not more than 6 years after act unless discovery prevented by fraudulent conduct of defendant; disability except minority tolls statute for 5 years but in no case after 1 year from removal of disability; minors have 12 years to bring suit.
Ohio	Ohio Revised Code Annotated, §2305.11	Within 1 year after the accrual except if before the 1 year expires the plaintiff gives written notice then suit may be brought within 180 days of notice but in no event after 4 years from act; disability tolls statute.

JURISDICTION	STATUTE	APPLICABLE PROVISION
Oklahoma	Oklahoma Statutes Annotated, Title 76, §18; Title 12, §96	Within 2 years from discovery or reasonable discoverability and medical injury suites brought more than 3 years from act shall have limited recovery; disability at time of injury tolls statute until 1 year after disability ends; minors under 12 must sue within 7 years; minors over 12 must sue within 1 year after attaining majority but in no event less than 2 years from date of injury; incompetents must sue within 7 years of injury unless adjudged incompetent then within 1 year after adjudication but in no event less than 2 years from date of injury.
Oregon	Oregon Revised Statutes, § 12.110; 160	Within 2 years from discovery or reasonable discoverability but not more than 5 years from act unless fraud; if fraud, 2 years from discovery or reasonable discovery; if minor or legal disability at time of injury then 5 years from accrual or 1 year after disability ends.
Pennsylvania	Pennsylvania Statutes Annotated, Title 42, §5524; Title 40, §1301.605	Within 2 years; if medical injury claim filed after 4 years from act, claim will be defended and paid by Medical Professional Liability Catastrophe Fund.
Rhode Island	Rhode Island General Laws, §9-1-14-1	Within 3 years from act or 3 years from discovery or reasonable discoverability; if minor or incompetent when injured then 3 years from removal of disability.
South Carolina	South Carolina Code Annotated, §15-3-545	Within 3 years from discovery or reasonable discoverability but not more than 6 years after act; foreign object within 2 years of discovery; if minor then statute is tolled for 7 years but not more than 1 year after majority.
South Dakota	South Dakota Codified Laws Annotated, §15-2-14.1	Within 2 years from act.
Tennessee	Tennessee Code Annotated, §29-26-116	Within 1 year from discovery but no more than 3 years from act unless fraud; if foreign object then 1 year from discovery.
Texas	Texas Revised Statutes Annotated, Article 4590i, §10.01	Within 2 years from occurrence; minor under 12 has until 14th birthday to sue otherwise applies to all regardless of minority or disability.

JURISDICTION	STATUTE	APPLICABLE PROVISION
Utah	Utah Code Annotated, §78-14-4	Within 2 years from discovery or discoverability but not more than 4 years from act; if foreign object or fraud then 1 year from discovery; statute applies regardless of minority or disability.
Vermont	Vermont Statutes Annotated, Title 12, §521	Within 3 years from act or 2 years from discovery or discoverability but no more than 7 years from act; no limitations if fraud; foreign object then 2 years from discovery.
Virginia	Virginia Code, §8.01-243	Within 2 years from accrual or 1 year from discovery or reasonable discovery; if foreign object then 1 year from discovery or reasonable discovery unless fraud or concealment; if infant then within 5 years of accrual but in no event beyond 10 years from accrual.
Washington	Washington Revised Code Annotated, §4.16.350	Within 3 years from act or 1 year from discovery or reasonable discoverability but no more than 8 years after act; fraud, concealment or foreign object tolls statute.
West Virginia	West Virginia Code, §55-7B-4	Within 2 years of injury or 2 years of discovery or reasonable discoverability, whichever occurs last but in no event longer than 10 years after date of injury; minor under 10 within 2 years of injury or by 12th birthday whichever provides a longer period; statute is tolled if fraud or concealment prevents discovery.
Wisconsin	Wisconsin Statutes Annotated, §893.55	Within 3 years from injury or 1 year from discovery or reasonable discoverability; if concealment or foreign object then 1 year from discovery or reasonable discoverability but in no event more than 5 years from act; minors must bring suit by age of 10 or under statute, whichever is later.
Wyoming	Wyoming Statutes, §1-3-107	Within 2 years from act but if discovered in 2nd year plaintiff gets 6 month extension; if discovery after 2 years, plaintiff has 2 years from discovery; 1 year after removal of disability; minor must file by 8th birthday or 2 years from act.

Source: Compendium of Selected State Laws Governing Medical Injury Claims, U.S. Department of Health and Human Services, Agency for Health Care Policy and Research, 1993.

APPENDIX 8:
SAMPLE PRODUCT LIABILITY COMPLAINT

[NAME OF COURT]

[CAPTION OF CASE] [FILE INDEX NUMBER]

COMPLAINT

Plaintiff, by his attorney, [name of attorney], complaining of the defendant, alleges, as follows:

FIRST: Plaintiff is a resident of the City, County and State of New York.

SECOND: Upon information and belief at all times hereinafter mentioned the defendant was and still is a domestic corporation, duly organized and existing under and by virtue of the laws of the State of New York.

FOR A FIRST CAUSE OF ACTION

THIRD: Upon information and belief, the defendant corporation is, and for approximately 10 years prior to March 7th, 2000, has been, engaged in the business of the manufacture and sale of bicycles to ultimate consumers such as the plaintiff and did, in fact, manufacture the bicycle owned and operated by the plaintiff.

FOURTH: Defendant designed, tested, manufactured, sold and promoted the bicycle, known as Model Number XZY123.

FIFTH: On March 7, 2000, plaintiff purchased one of defendant's bicycles, known as Model Number XYZ123.

SIXTH: On July 4, 2000, plaintiff was operating this bicycle when the handle bars cracked and dislodged from the main frame of the bicycle.

SEVENTH: Defendant was careless in the design, testing, inspection, manufacture, distribution, labeling, sale and promotion of said bicycle.

EIGHTH: As a result of defendant's conduct, plaintiff was seriously injured and has sustained general and special damages.

SECOND CAUSE OF ACTION

NINTH: Plaintiff repeats and reiterates each allegation contained in paragraphs 1 through 8 of this complaint.

TENTH: The bicycle was defective in that the handlebars broke and dislodged from the main frame as a result of which defendant has become strictly liable to plaintiff.

ELEVENTH: By reason of the foregoing, the plaintiff has been damaged in the sum of Two Hundred Fifty ($150,000) Dollars.

WHEREFORE, plaintiff demands judgment against defendant in the amount of One Hundred Fifty ($150,000) Dollars; costs and disbursements of this action; and any other relief the Court deems appropriate.

PLEASE TAKE NOTICE, that pursuant to the CPLR, you are required to serve a copy of your answer within 20 days after the service of this Complaint.

Dated:

[Signature Line]

[Name of Attorney]

Attorney for Plaintiff

[Attorney's Address]

[Attorney's Telephone Number]

APPENDIX 9:
SAMPLE COMPLAINT TO RECOVER
NO-FAULT INSURANCE BENEFITS

[NAME OF COURT]

[CAPTION OF CASE] [FILE INDEX NUMBER]

COMPLAINT

The plaintiff, complaining of the defendant, by his attorney, [name of attorney] herein states the following:

1. Upon information and belief, the defendant is a foreign insurance corporation doing business in the State of New York. under the laws of the State of New York.

2. At all times hereinafter mentioned, the defendant was and still is engaged in the business of insuring automobiles and the drivers thereof against certain hazards, including personal injuries.

3. On [date] the defendant issued and delivered an insurance policy, Policy No.___, to its insured, [name of insured].

4. Said insurance policy contains an agreement to insure the driver of the insured vehicle for "Basic Economic Loss" as described in Insurance Law § 5102(a), up to the limit set forth in the policy.

5. On or about [date of accident], at about [time of accident], and while the policy was in full force and effect, the plaintiff was injured while driving the insured vehicle with the permission of the insured, [name of insured].

6. Solely as a result of the accident and injuries sustained, the plaintiff suffered "Basic Economic Loss", hereinafter referred to as "First Party Benefits".

7. The plaintiff and/or the insured gave notice to the defendant as soon as practicable after the aforementioned accident.

8. On or about [date], some four (#) months after the accident, the defendant sent a letter enclosing a copy of its No-Fault application form to the plaintiff.

9. The plaintiff has completed and properly executed all the forms supplied by the defendant and has submitted the required proof of his claim therewith.

10. Demand has been made of the defendant by the plaintiff for "First Party Benefits" and the defendant has not paid the sum or any part thereof.

11. More than thirty (30) days have elapsed since the accident and since the date of plaintiffs demand. Payments are therefore overdue.

12. That as a result of the above, the plaintiff incurred an uncompensated loss of wages, medical bills, interest, attorneys' fees and was otherwise injured and damaged in the sum of _____ ($_____) Dollars.

WHEREFORE, plaintiff demands judgment against the defendant in the sum of _____ ($_____) Dollars, plus interest, the costs and disbursements of this action, and such other and further relief as the Court deems just and proper.

Dated:

[Signature Line]

      [Name of Attorney]

      Attorney for Plaintiff

      [Attorney's Address]

      [Attorney's Telephone Number]

APPENDIX 10:
SAMPLE COMPLAINT FOR PERSONAL INJURY IN AN AUTOMOBILE ACCIDENT UNDER NEW YORK STATE LAW

[NAME OF COURT]

[CAPTION OF CASE]

COMPLAINT

INDEX NO:

The plaintiff, complaining of the defendant by his attorney, [name of attorney] & , herein states the following:

1. That at all times hereinafter mentioned, the plaintiff was, and still is, a resident of the City of [name], County of [name], New York.

2. That upon information and belief, at all times hereinafter mentioned, and at the time of the commencement of this action, the defendant was, and still is, a resident of the City of [name], County of [name], New York.

3. That upon information and belief, the defendant was, and still is, the owner and operator of [identify defendant's vehicle].

4. That at all times hereinafter mentioned, the plaintiff was lawfully the operator of [identify plaintiff's vehicle].

5. That upon information and belief, at all the times hereinafter mentioned, [identify road upon which accident occurred, e.g. Main Street located at the intersection of Spring Street, in the County of Queens, New York, was a public highway running in a general north-south direction].

6. That on or about [date and time], plaintiff was lawfully operating his vehicle [describe accident, e.g., which was traveling in a southerly direction along Main Street, when the automobile owned and operated by the defendant, traveling in a northerly direction along Main Street collided with the plaintiff's vehicle while making a left turn across Main Street at the intersection of Spring Street], causing the injuries to the plaintiff.

7. That the accident and the injuries resulting to the plaintiff were caused solely by reason of the negligence of the defendant.

8. That the defendant was negligent, reckless, and careless at that time and place in that defendant turned left across the road without signalling and without giving any warning of his intention to so turn left across the road; in that the defendant was not paying proper attention to the operation or progress of the vehicle operated by the plaintiff; in that the defendant failed to keep a proper lookout before turning left across the road for danger reasonably to be apprehended and/or to observe and heed road and traffic conditions then and there existing; in that the defendant failed to exercise due and proper care and diligence to avoid the accident; in that defendant was otherwise generally careless and negligent.

9. That as a result of the collision and accident, plaintiff suffered great bodily injuries, and he became sick, sore, lame and disabled and has remained sick, sore, lame and disabled since the accident and has suffered great pain and agony and is informed and believes that he will continue to suffer for a long time to come, and that the injuries are permanent; that the plaintiff has been unable to carry on his duties for some time and believes that in the future he will be unable to, and hindered in, carrying out his duties.

10. That by reason of the foregoing, the plaintiff has been damaged in the sum of [set forth dollar amount of claim].

Plaintiff must set forth the allegations which take this claim out of no-fault using either paragraph 11-A or 11-B, whichever is applicable to the facts:

11-A. That as a result of the foregoing, the plaintiff has sustained a serious injury, as defined in subsection (d) of section 5102 of the Insurance Law of the State of New York.

11-B. That as a result of the foregoing, the plaintiff has sustained economic loss greater than basic economic loss, as defined in subsection (a) of section 5102 of the Insurance Law of the State of New York.

WHEREFORE, plaintiff demands judgment against the defendant in the sum of [set forth dollar amount of claim, plus interest, the costs and disbursements of this action, and such other and further relief as the Court deems just and proper.

Dated:

[Signature Line]

    [Name of Attorney]

    Attorney for Plaintiff

    [Attorney's Address]

    [Attorney's Telephone Number]

APPENDIX 11:
APPLICABLE SECTIONS OF THE
RESTATEMENT SECOND OF THE LAW OF
TORTS CONCERNING DEFAMATION

Section 558: Elements Stated

To create liability for defamation there must be:

(a) a false and defamatory statement concerning another;

(b) an unprivileged publication to a third party;

(c) fault amounting at least to negligence on the part of the publisher; and

(d) either actionability of the statement irrespective of special harm or the existence of special harm caused by the publication.

Section 559: Defamatory Communication Defined

A communication is defamatory if it tends so to harm the reputation of another as to lower him in the estimation of the community or to deter third persons from associating or dealing with him.

Section 560: Defamation Of Deceased Persons

One who publishes defamatory matter concerning a deceased person is not liable either to the estate of the person or to his descendants or relatives.

Section 568: Libel And Slander Distinguished

(1) Libel consists of the publication of defamatory matter by written or printed words, by its embodiment in physical form or by any other form of

communication that has the potentially harmful qualities characteristic of written or printed words.

(2) Slander consists of the publication of defamatory matter by spoken words, transitory gestures or by any form of communication other than those stated in Subsection (1).

(3) The area of dissemination, the deliberate and premeditated character of its publication and the persistence of the defamation are factors to be considered in determining whether a publication is a libel rather than a slander.

Section 569: Liability Without Proof Of Special Harm—Libel

One who falsely publishes matter defamatory of another in such a manner as to make the publication a libel is subject to liability to the other although no special harm results from the publication.

Section 570: Liability Without Proof Of Special Harm—Slander

One who publishes matter defamatory to another in such a manner as to make the publication a slander is subject to liability to the other although no special harm results if the publication imputes to the other:

(a) a criminal offense, as stated in §571, or

(b) a loathsome disease, as stated in §572, or

(c) matter incompatible with his business, trade, profession, or office, as stated in §573, or

(d) serious sexual misconduct, as stated in §574.

Section 571: Slanderous Imputations Of Criminal Conduct

One who publishes a slander that imputes to another conduct constituting a criminal offense is subject to liability to the other without proof of special harm if the offense imputed is of a type which, if committed in the place of publication, would be:

(a) punishable by imprisonment in a state or federal institution, or

(b) regarded by public opinion as involving moral turpitude.

Section 572: Slanderous Imputations Of Loathsome Disease

One who publishes a slander that imputes to another an existing venereal disease or other loathsome and communicable disease is subject to liability without proof of special harm.

Section 573: Slanderous Imputations Affecting Business, Trade, Profession Or Office

One who publishes a slander that ascribes to another conduct, characteristics or a condition that would adversely affect his fitness for the proper conduct of his lawful business, trade or profession, or of his public or private office, whether honorary or for profit, is subject to liability without proof of special harm.

Section 574: Slanderous Imputations Of Sexual Misconduct

One who publishes a slander that imputes serious sexual misconduct to another is subject to liability to the other without proof of special harm.

Section 575: Slander Creating Liability Because Of Special Harm

One who publishes a slander that, although not actionable per se, is the legal cause of special harm to the person defamed, is subject to liability to him.

Section 576: Harm Caused By Repetition

The publication of a libel or slander is a legal cause of any special harm resulting from its repetition by a third person if, but only if:

(a) the third person was privileged to repeat it, or

(b) the repetition was authorized or intended by the original defamer, or

(c) the repetition was reasonably to be expected.

Section 577a: Single And Multiple Publications

(1) Except as stated in Subsections (2) and (3), each of several communications to a third person by the same defamer is a separate publication.

(2) A single communication heard at the same time by two or more third persons is a single publication.

(3) Any one edition of a book or newspaper, or any one radio or television broadcast, exhibition of a motion picture or similar aggregate communication is a single publication.

(4) As to any single publication:

(a) only one action for damages can be maintained;

(b) all damages suffered in all jurisdictions can be recovered in the one action; and

(c) a judgment for or against the plaintiff upon the merits of any action for damages bars any other action for damages between the same parties in all jurisdictions.

Section 578: Liability Of Republisher

Except as to those who only deliver or transmit defamation published by a third person, one who repeats or otherwise republishes defamatory matter is subject to liability as if he had originally published it.

Section 580a: Defamation Of Public Official Or Public Figure

One who publishes a false and defamatory communication concerning a public official or public figure in regard to his conduct, fitness or role in that capacity is subject to liability, if, but only if, he:

(a) knows that the statement is false and that it defames the other person, or

(b) acts in reckless disregard of these matters.

Section 580b: Defamation Of Private Person

One who publishes a false and defamatory communication concerning a private person, or concerning a public official or public figure in relation to a purely private matter not affecting his conduct, fitness or role in his public capacity, is subject to liability, if, but only if, he:

(a) knows that the statement is false and that it defames the other,

(b) acts in reckless disregard of these matters, or

(c) acts negligently in failing to ascertain them.

Section 581a: True Statements

One who publishes a defamatory statement of fact is not subject to liability for defamation if the statement is true.

TITLE A: CONSENT

Section 583: General Principle

Except as stated in §584, the consent of another to the publication of defamatory matter concerning him is a complete defense to his action for defamation.

TITLE B: ABSOLUTE PRIVILEGE IRRESPECTIVE OF CONSENT

Section 585: Judicial Officers

A judge or other officer performing a judicial function is absolutely privileged to publish defamatory matter in the performance of the function if the publication has some relation to the matter before him.

TITLE B: ABSOLUTE PRIVILEGE IRRESPECTIVE OF CONSENT

Section 586: Attorneys At Law

An attorney at law is absolutely privileged to publish defamatory matter concerning another in communications preliminary to a proposed judicial proceeding, or in the institution of, or during the course and as a part of, a judicial proceeding in which he participates as counsel, if it has some relation to the proceeding.

TITLE B: ABSOLUTE PRIVILEGE IRRESPECTIVE OF CONSENT

Section 587: Parties To Judicial Proceedings

A party to a private litigation or a private prosecutor or defendant in a criminal prosecution is absolutely privileged to publish defamatory matter concerning another in communications preliminary to a proposed judicial proceeding, or in the institution of or during the course and as a part of, a judicial proceeding in which he participates, if the matter has some relation to the proceeding.

TITLE B: ABSOLUTE PRIVILEGE IRRESPECTIVE OF CONSENT

Section 588: Witnesses In Judicial Proceedings

A witness is absolutely privileged to publish defamatory matter concerning another in communications preliminary to a proposed judicial proceeding or as a part of a judicial proceeding in which he is testifying, if it has some relation to the proceeding.

TITLE B: ABSOLUTE PRIVILEGE IRRESPECTIVE OF CONSENT

Section 589: Jurors

A member of a grand or petit jury is absolutely privileged to publish defamatory matter concerning another in the performance of his function as a juror, if the defamatory matter has some relation to the proceedings in which he is acting as juror.

TITLE B: ABSOLUTE PRIVILEGE IRRESPECTIVE OF CONSENT

Section 590: Legislators

A member of the Congress of the United States or of a State or local legislative body is absolutely privileged to publish defamatory matter concerning another in the performance of his legislative functions.

TITLE B: ABSOLUTE PRIVILEGE IRRESPECTIVE OF CONSENT

Section 590a: Witnesses In Legislative Proceedings

A witness is absolutely privileged to publish defamatory matter as part of a legislative proceeding in which he is testifying or in communications preliminary to the proceeding, if the matter has some relation to the proceeding.

TITLE B: ABSOLUTE PRIVILEGE IRRESPECTIVE OF CONSENT

Section 591: Executive And Administrative Officers

An absolute privilege to publish defamatory matter concerning another in communications made in the performance of his official duties exists for:

(a) any executive or administrative officer of the United States; or

(b) a governor or other superior executive officer of a state.

TITLE B: ABSOLUTE PRIVILEGE IRRESPECTIVE OF CONSENT

Section 592: Husband And Wife

A husband or a wife is absolutely privileged to publish to the other spouse defamatory matter concerning a third person.

TITLE B: ABSOLUTE PRIVILEGE IRRESPECTIVE OF CONSENT

Section 592a: Publication Required By Law

One who is required by law to publish defamatory matter is absolutely privileged to publish it.

Section 594: Protection Of The Publisher's Interest

An occasion makes a publication conditionally privileged if the circumstances induce a correct or reasonable belief that:

(a) there is information that affects a sufficiently important interest of the publisher; and

(b) the recipient's knowledge of the defamatory matter will be of service in the lawful protection of the interest.

Section 595: Protection Of Interest Of Recipient Or A Third Person

(1) An occasion makes a publication conditionally privileged if the circumstances induce a correct or reasonable belief that:

(a) there is information that affects a sufficiently important interest of the recipient or a third person, and

(b) the recipient is one to whom the publisher is under a legal duty to publish the defamatory matter or is a person to whom its publication is otherwise within the generally accepted standards of decent conduct.

(2) In determining whether a publication is within generally accepted standards of decent conduct it is an important factor that:

(a) the publication is made in response to a request rather than volunteered by the publisher, or

(b) a family or other relationship exists between the parties.

Section 596: Common Interest

An occasion makes a publication conditionally privileged if the circumstances lead any one of several persons having a common interest in a particular subject matter correctly or reasonably to believe that there is information that another sharing the common interest is entitled to know.

Section 597: Family Relationships

(1) An occasion makes a publication conditionally privileged if the circumstances induce a correct or reasonable belief that:

(a) there is information that affects the well-being of a member of the immediate family of the publisher, and

(b) the recipient's knowledge of the defamatory matter will be of service in the lawful protection of the well-being of the member of the family.

(2) An occasion makes a publication conditionally privileged when the circumstances induce a correct or reasonable belief that:

(a) there is information that affects the well-being of a member of the immediate family of the recipient or of a third person, and

(b) the recipient's knowledge of the defamatory matter will be of service in the lawful protection of the well-being of the member of the family, and

(c) the recipient has requested the publication of the defamatory matter or is a person to whom its publication is otherwise within generally accepted standards of decent conduct.

Section 598: Communication To One Who May Act In The Public Interest

An occasion makes a publication conditionally privileged if the circumstances induce a correct or reasonable belief that:

(a) there is information that affects a sufficiently important public interest, and

(b) the public interest requires the communication of the defamatory matter to a public officer or a private citizen who is authorized or privileged to take action if the defamatory matter is true.

Section 598a: Inferior State Officers

An occasion makes a publication conditionally privileged if an inferior administrative officer of a state or any of its subdivisions who is not entitled to an absolute privilege makes a defamatory communication required or permitted in the performance of his official duties.

Section 600: Knowledge Of Falsity Or Reckless Disregard As To Truth

Except as stated in §682, one who upon an occasion giving rise to a conditional privilege publishes false and defamatory matter concerning another abuses the privilege if he

(a) knows the matter to be false, or

(b) acts in reckless disregard as to its truth or falsity.

Section 602: Publication Of A Defamatory Rumor

One who upon an occasion giving rise to a conditional privilege publishes a defamatory rumor or suspicion concerning another does not abuse the privilege, even if he knows or believes the rumor or suspicion to be false, if:

(a) he states the defamatory matter as rumor or suspicion and not as fact, and

(b) the relation of the parties, the importance of the interests affected, and the harm likely to be done make the publication reasonable.

Section 603: Purpose Of The Privilege

One who upon an occasion giving rise to a conditional privilege publishes defamatory matter concerning another abuses the privilege if he does not act for the purpose of protecting the interest for the protection of which the privilege is given.

Section 604: Excessive Publication

One who, upon an occasion giving rise to a conditional privilege for the publication of defamatory matter to a particular person or persons, knowingly publishes the matter to a person to whom its publication is not otherwise privileged, abuses the privilege unless he reasonably believes that the publication is a proper means of communicating the defamatory matter to the person to whom its publication is privileged.

Section 605: Necessity For Publication And Purpose Of Privilege

One who upon an occasion giving rise to a conditional privilege publishes defamatory matter concerning another, abuses the privilege if he does not reasonably believe the matter to be necessary to accomplish the purpose for which the privilege is given.

Section 613: Burden Of Proof

(1) In an action for defamation the plaintiff has the burden of proving, when the issue is properly raised:

(a) the defamatory character of the communication,

(b) its publication by the defendant,

(c) its application to the plaintiff,

(d) the recipient's understanding of its defamatory meaning,

(e) the recipient's understanding of it as intended to be applied to the plaintiff,

(f) special harm resulting to the plaintiff from its publication,

(g) the defendant's negligence, reckless disregard or knowledge regarding the truth or falsity and the defamatory character of the communication, and

(h) the abuse of a conditional privilege.

(2) In an action for defamation the defendant has the burden of proving, when the issue is properly raised, the presence of the circumstances necessary for the existence of a privilege to publish the defamatory communication.

Section 614: Determination Of Meaning And Defamatory Character Of Communication

(1) The court determines:

(a) whether a communication is capable of bearing a particular meaning, and

(b) whether that meaning is defamatory.

(2) The jury determines whether a communication, capable of a defamatory meaning, was so understood by its recipient.

Section 615: Determination Of Slander Actionable Per Se

(1) The court determines whether a crime, a disease or a type of sexual misconduct imputed by spoken language is of such a character as to make the slander actionable per se.

(2) Subject to the control of the court whenever the issue arises, the jury determines whether spoken language imputes to another conduct, characteristics or a condition incompatible with the proper conduct of his business, trade, profession or office.

Section 616: Determination Of Damages

The Court determines what items of harm suffered by the plaintiff as the result of the publication of the defamatory matter may be considered by the jury in assessing damages; the jury determines the amount of damages to be awarded for those items.

Section 617: Publication, Truth And Defendant's Fault

Subject to the control of the court whenever the issue arises, the jury determines whether:

(a) the defamatory matter was published of and concerning the plaintiff;

(b) the matter was true or false; and

(c) the defendant had the requisite fault in regard to the truth or falsity of the matter and its defamatory character.

Section 619: Privileges

(1) The court determines whether the occasion upon which the defendant published the defamatory matter gives rise to a privilege.

(2) Subject to the control of the court whenever the issue arises, the jury determines whether the defendant abused a conditional privilege.

Section 620: Nominal Damages

One who is liable for a slander actionable per se or for a libel is liable for at least nominal damages.

Section 621: General Damages

One who is liable for a defamatory communication is liable for the proved, actual harm caused to the reputation of the person defamed.

Section 622: Special Harm As Affecting The Measure Of Recovery

One Who Is Liable For Either A Slander Actionable Per Se Or A Libel Is Also Liable For Any Special Harm Legally Caused By The Defamatory Publication.

Section 622a: Legal Causation Of Special Harm

Defamation is a legal cause of special harm to the person defamed if:

(a) it is a substantial factor in bringing about the harm, and

(b) there is no rule of law relieving the publisher from liability because of the manner in which the publication has resulted in the harm.

Section 623: Emotional Distress And Resulting Bodily Harm

One who is liable to another for a libel or slander is liable also for emotional distress and bodily harm that is proved to have been caused by the defamatory publication.

APPENDIX 12:
SAMPLE DEFAMATION COMPLAINT

[NAME OF COURT]

[CAPTION OF CASE] [FILE INDEX NUMBER]

COMPLAINT

Plaintiff, by her attorney, [name of attorney], complaining of the defendant, alleges, as follows:

FIRST: Plaintiff, John Doe, is a resident of the City, County and State of New York.

SECOND: Upon information and belief at all times hereinafter mentioned the defendant was and still is a domestic corporation, duly organized and existing under and by virtue of the laws of the State of New York.

THIRD: Upon information and belief, the defendant corporation owned and published a certain magazine known as the [name of publication].

FOURTH: Upon information and belief, the magazine was published daily and enjoyed a large sale and circulation to the public in the County of Westchester, State of New York.

FIFTH: Upon information and belief, at all times hereinafter mentioned, the defendant, James Smith, was a writer employed by the defendant magazine.

SIXTH: On the 27th day of March, 2000, the defendant magazine published and circulated, and the defendant writer participated in the preparation and publication of, a false, defamatory, malicious and libelous article concerning the plaintiff, a copy of which is attached hereto as

Exhibit A, which article contains, among other things, the following statement:

> "John Doe, residing at 123 Main Street, White Plains, New York, was arrested on Saturday night for the possession and sale of drugs to minors."

SEVENTH: Upon information and belief, at the time of the aforesaid publication, the defendants were actuated by actual malice in that the defendants knew that the article and the information contained therein concerning the plaintiff was false and untrue and/or was published with reckless and wanton disregard of whether they were false and untrue.

EIGHTH: As a result of the publication of this article, and the acts of the defendants in connection with its publication, the plaintiff has been held up to public contempt, ridicule, disgrace and has suffered great mental pain and anguish, and has been irreparably injured in his good name, business reputation, and social standing, and has lost the esteem and respect of his friends, acquaintances, business associates, and of the public generally.

NINTH: By reason of the foregoing, plaintiff has been greatly injured and damaged and, in addition, are entitled to punitive damages against the defendants, all in the sum of Three Hundred Thousand ($300,000) Dollars.

WHEREFORE, plaintiff demands judgment against defendant in the amount of Three Hundred Thousand ($300,000) Dollars; costs and disbursements of this action; and any other relief the Court deems appropriate.

PLEASE TAKE NOTICE, that pursuant to the CPLR, you are required to serve a copy of your answer within 20 days after the service of this Complaint.

Dated:

[Signature Line]

[Name of Attorney]

Attorney for Plaintiff

[Attorney's Address]

[Attorney's Telephone Number]

APPENDIX 13:
STATE STATUTES OF LIMITATIONS FOR DEFAMATION CLAIMS

STATE	LIMITATIONS PERIOD
Alabama	2 YEARS
Alaska	2 YEARS
Arizona	1 YEAR
Arkansas	1 YEAR FOR SLANDER, 3 YEARS FOR LIBEL
California	1 YEAR
Colorado	1 YEAR
Connecticut	2 YEARS
Delaware	2 YEARS
District of Columbia	1 YEAR
Florida	2 YEARS
Georgia	1 YEAR
Hawaii	2 YEARS
Idaho	2 YEARS
Illinois	1 YEAR
Indiana	2 YEARS
Iowa	2 YEARS
Kansas	1 YEAR
Kentucky	1 YEAR

STATE	LIMITATIONS PERIOD
Louisiana	1 YEAR
Maine	2 YEARS
Maryland	1 YEAR
Massachusetts	3 YEARS
Michigan	1 YEAR
Minnesota	2 YEARS
Mississippi	1 YEAR
Missouri	2 YEARS
Montana	2 YEARS
Nebraska	1 YEAR
Nevada	2 YEARS
New Hampshire	3 YEARS
New Jersey	1 YEAR
New Mexico	3 YEARS
New York	1 YEAR
North Carolina	1 YEAR
North Dakota	2 YEARS
Ohio	1 YEAR
Oklahoma	1 YEAR
Oregon	1 YEAR
Pennsylvania	1 YEAR
Rhode Island	1 YEAR FOR SLANDER, 3 YEARS FOR LIBEL
South Carolina	2 YEARS
South Dakota	2 YEARS
Tennessee	6 MONTHS FOR SLANDER, 1 YEAR FOR LIBEL
Texas	1 YEAR
Utah	1 YEAR
Vermont	3 YEARS
Virginia	2 YEARS

STATE	LIMITATIONS PERIOD
Washington	2 YEARS
West Virginia	1 YEAR
Wisconsin	2 YEARS
Wyoming	1 YEAR

APPENDIX 14:
STATE WRONGFUL DEATH STATUTES

JURISDICTION	STATUTE
Alabama	Code of Alabama § 10-5-410
Alaska	Alaska Statutes § 09.55.580
Arizona	Arizona Revised Statutes § 12-542
Arkansas	Arkansas Statutes Annotated § 27-906
California	California Code of Civil Procedure § 377
Colorado	Colorado Revised Statutes § 13-21-201
Connecticut	Connecticut General Statutes Annotated § 52-555
Delaware	Delaware Code Annotated Title 10 § 3701
District of Columbia	District of Columbia Code Title 16 § 2702
Florida	Florida Statutes Annotated § 768.20
Georgia	Code of Georgia § 51-4-2
Hawaii	Hawaii Revised Statutes § 666-3
Idaho	Idaho Code § 5-310
Illinois	Illinois Revised Statutes Chapter 70§ 2
Indiana	Indiana Code Annotated § 34-4-2-1
Iowa	Code of Iowa § 611.20
Kansas	Kansas Statutes§ 60-1902
Kentucky	Kentucky Revised Statutes § 411.130
Louisiana	Louisiana Revised Statutes § 2315
Maine	Maine Revised Statutes Annotated Title 18A § 2-804

JURISDICTION	STATUTE
Maryland	Maryland Courts & Judicial Procedure Code Annotated § 3-904
Massachusetts	Annotated Laws of Massachusetts Chapter 229 § 2
Michigan	Michigan Compiled Laws § 600.2922
Minnesota	Minnesota Statutes § 573.02
Mississippi	Mississippi Code Annotated § 11-7-13
Missouri	Annotated Missouri Statutes § 537.080
Montana	Revised Montana Code Annotated § 27-1-512
Nebraska	Revised Statutes of Nebraska § 30-810
Nevada	Nevada Revised Statutes § 41.080
New Hampshire	New Hampshire Revised Statutes Annotated § 556:12
New Jersey	New Jersey Statutes Annotated § 2A:31-1
New Mexico	New Mexico Statutes Annotated§ 41-2-1
New York	New York EPTL § 5-4.1
North Carolina	General Statutes of North Carolina § 28A-18-2
North Dakota	North Dakota Century Code § 32-21-03
Ohio	Ohio Revised Code Annotated § 2125.02
Oklahoma	Oklahoma Statutes Annotated Title 12§ 1053
Oregon	Oregon Revised Statutes § 30.020
Pennsylvania	Pennsylvania Statutes Annotated Title 42§ 8301
Rhode Island	General Laws of Rhode Island § 10-7-2
South Carolina	Code of Laws of South Carolina § 15-51-20
South Dakota	South Dakota Codified Laws Annotated § 21-5-5
Tennessee	Tennessee Code Annotated § 20-5-106
Texas	Texas Revised Civil Statutes Annotated Article 5525
Utah	Utah Code Annotated § 78-11-6
Vermont	Vermont Statutes Annotated Title 14 § 1491
Virginia	Code of Virginia Annotated § 8.01-56
Washington	Washington Revised Code Annotated § 4.20.010

JURISDICTION	STATUTE
West Virginia	West Virginia Code § 55-7-6
Wisconsin	Wisconsin Statutes Annotated § 895.04
Wyoming	Wyoming Statutes § 1.38-102

APPENDIX 15:
THE UNIFORM ARBITRATION ACT

**Act Relating to Arbitration and to Make Uniform the Law
With Reference Thereto**

Section 1: Validity of Arbitration Agreement

A written agreement to submit any existing controversy to arbitration or a
provision in a written contract to submit to arbitration any controversy
thereafter arising between the parties is valid, enforceable and irrevocable,
save upon such grounds as exist at law or in equity for the revocation of
any contract. This act also applies to arbitration agreements between employers and employees or between their respective representatives unless
otherwise provided in the agreement.

Section 2: Proceedings to Compel or Stay Arbitration

(a) On application of a party showing an agreement described in Section 1, and the opposing party's refusal to arbitrate, the Court shall order the parties to proceed with arbitration, but if the opposing party denies the existence of the agreement to arbitrate, the Court shall proceed
summarily to the determination of the issue so raised and shall order
arbitration if found for the moving party, otherwise, the application
shall be denied.

(b) On application, the courts may stay an arbitration proceeding commenced or threatened on a showing that there is no agreement to arbitrate. Such an issue, when in substantial and bona fide dispute, shall
be forthwith and summarily tried and the stay ordered if found for the
moving party. If found for the opposing party, the court shall order the
parties to proceed to arbitration.

(c) If an issue referable to arbitration under the alleged agreement is involved in action or proceeding pending in a court having jurisdiction to

hear applications under subdivision (a) of this Section, the application shall be made therein. Otherwise and subject to Section 18, the application may be made in any court of competent jurisdiction.

(d) Any action or proceeding involving an issue subject to arbitration shall be stayed if an order for arbitration or an application therefore has been made under this section or, if the issue is severable, the stay may be with respect thereto only. When the application is made in such action or proceeding, the order for arbitration shall include such stay.

(e) An order for arbitration shall not be refused on the ground that the claim in issue lacks merit or bona fides or because any fault or grounds for the claim sought to be arbitrated have not been shown.

Section 3: Appointment of Arbitrators by Courts

If the arbitration agreement provides a method of appointment of arbitrators, this method shall be followed. In the absence thereof, or if the agreed method fails or for any reason cannot be followed, or when an arbitrator appointed fails or is unable to act and his successor has not been duly appointed, the court on application of a party shall appoint one or more arbitrators. An arbitrator so appointed has all the powers of one specifically named in the agreement.

Section 4: Majority Action by Arbitrators

The powers of the arbitrators may be exercised by a majority unless otherwise provided by the agreement or by this act.

Section 5: Hearing

Unless otherwise provided by the agreement:

(a) The arbitrators shall appoint a time and place for the hearing and cause notification to the parties to be served personally or by registered mail not less than five days before the hearing. Appearance at the hearing waives such notice. The arbitrators may adjourn the hearing from time to time as necessary and, on request of a party and for good cause, or upon their own motion may postpone the hearing to a time not later than the date fixed by the agreement for making the award unless the parties consent to a later date. The arbitrators may hear and determine the controversy upon the evidence produced notwithstanding the failure of a party duly notified to appear. The court on application may direct the arbitrators to proceed promptly with the hearing and determination of the controversy.

(b) The parties are entitled to be heard, to present evidence material to the controversy and to cross-examine witnesses appearing at the hearing.

(c) The hearing shall be conducted by all the arbitrators but a majority may determine any question and render a final award. If, during the course of the hearing, an arbitrator for any reason ceases to act, the remaining arbitrator or arbitrators appointed to act as neutrals may continue with the hearing and determination of the controversy.

Section 6: Representation by Attorney

A party has the right to be represented by an attorney at any proceeding or hearing under this act. A waiver thereof prior to the proceeding or hearing is ineffective.

Section 7: Witnesses, Subpoenas, Depositions

(a) The arbitrators may issue or cause to be issued subpoenas for the attendance of witnesses and for the production of books, records, documents and other evidence, and shall have the power to administer oaths. Subpoenas so issued shall be served, and upon application to the Court by a party or the arbitrators, enforced, in the manner provided by law for the service and enforcement of subpoenas in a civil action.

(b) On application of a party and for use as evidence, the arbitrators may permit a deposition to be taken, in the manner and upon the terms designated by the arbitrators, of a witness who cannot be subpoenaed or is unable to attend the hearing.

(c) All provisions of law compelling a person under subpoena to testify are applicable.

(d) Fees for attendance as a witness shall be the same as for a witness in Court.

Section 8: Award

(a) The award shall be in writing and signed by the arbitrators joining in the award. The arbitrators shall deliver a copy to each party personally or by registered mail, or as provided in this agreement.

(b) An award shall be made within the time fixed therefor by the agreement or, if not so fixed, within such time as the court orders on application of a party. The parties may extend the time in writing either before or after the expiration thereof. A party waives the objection that an award was not made within the time required unless he notifies the arbitrators of his objection prior to the delivery of the award to him.

Section 9: Change of Award by Arbitrators

On application of a party or, if an application to the court is pending under Sections 11, 12, or 13, on submission to the arbitrators by the court under such conditions as the court may order, the arbitrators may modify or correct the award upon the grounds stated in paragraphs (1) and (3) of subdivision (a) of Section 13, or for the purpose of clarifying the award. The application shall be made within twenty days after delivery of the award to the applicant. Written notice thereof shall be given forthwith to the opposing party, stating he must serve his objection thereto if any, within ten days from the notice. The award so modified or corrected is subject to the provisions of Sections 11, 12 and 13.

Section 10: Fees and Expenses of Arbitration

Unless otherwise provided in the agreement to arbitrate, the arbitrators' expenses and fees, together with other expenses, not including counsel fees, incurred in the conduct of the arbitration, shall be paid as provided in the award.

Section 11: Confirmation of an Award

(a) Upon application of a party, the court shall vacate an award where:

(1) The award was procured by corruption, fraud or other undue means;

(2) There was evident partiality by an arbitrator appointed as neutral, or corruption in any of the arbitrators or misconduct prejudicing the rights of any party;

(3) The arbitrators exceeded their powers;

(4) The arbitrators refused to postpone the hearing upon sufficient cause being shown therefor or refused to hear evidence material to the controversy or otherwise so conducted the hearing contrary to the provisions of Section 5, as to prejudice substantially the rights of a party; or

(5) There was no arbitration agreement and the issue was not adversely determined in proceedings under Section 2 and the party did not participate in the arbitration hearing without raising the objection;

But the fact that the relief was such that it could not or would not be granted by a court of law or equity is not ground for vacating or refusing to confirm the award.

(b) An application under this Section shall be made within ninety days after delivery of a copy of the award to the applicant, except that, if predicated upon corruption, fraud or other undue means, it shall be made within ninety days after such grounds are known or should have been known.

(c) In vacating the award on grounds other than stated in clause (5) of Subsection (a) the court may order a rehearing before new arbitrators chosen as provided in the agreement, or in the absence thereof, by the court in accordance with Section 3, or, if the award is vacated on grounds set forth in clauses (3), and (4) of Subsection (a) the court may order a rehearing before the arbitrators who made the award or their successors appointed in accordance with Section 3. The time within which the agreement requires the award to be made is applicable to the rehearing and commences from the date of the award.

(d) If the application to vacate is denied and no motion to modify or correct the award is pending, the court shall confirm the award.

Section 13: Modification or Correction of Award

(a) Upon application made within ninety days after delivery of a copy of the award to the applicant, the court shall modify or correct the award where:

(1) There was an evident miscalculation of figures or an evident mistake in the description of any person, thing or property referred to in the award;

(2) The arbitrators have awarded upon a matter not submitted to them and the award may be corrected without affecting the merits of the decision upon the issues submitted; or

(3) The award is imperfect in a matter of form, not affecting the merits of the controversy;

(b) If the application is granted, the court shall modify and correct the award so as to effects its intent and shall confirm the award as so modified and corrected. Otherwise, the court shall confirm the award as made.

(c) An application to modify or correct an award may be joined in the alternative with an application to vacate the award.

Section 14: Judgment or Decree on Award

Upon the granting of an order confirming, modifying or correcting an award, judgment or decree shall be entered in conformity therewith and be enforced as any other judgment or decree. Costs of the application and of the proceedings subsequent thereto, and disbursements may be awarded by the court.

Section 15: Judgment Roll, Docketing

(a) On entry of a judgment or decree, the clerk shall prepare the judgment roll consisting, to the extent filed, of the following:

(1) The agreement and each written extension of the time within which to make the award;

(2) The award;

(3) A copy of the order confirming, modifying or correcting the award; and

(4) A copy of the judgment or decree.

(b) The judgment or decree may be docketed as if rendered in an action.

Section 16: Applications to Court

Except as otherwise provided, an application to the court under this act shall be by motion and shall be heard in the manner and upon the notice provided by law or rule of court for the making and hearing of motions. Unless the parties have agreed otherwise, notice of an initial application for an order shall be served in the manner provided by law for the service of a summons and complaint.

Section 17: Court, Jurisdiction

The term "court" means any court of competent jurisdiction of this State. The making of an agreement described in Section 1 providing for arbitration in this State confers jurisdiction on the court to enforce the agreement under this act and to enter judgment on an award thereunder.

Section 18: Venue

An initial application shall be made to the court of the county in which the agreement provides the arbitration hearing shall be held or, if the hearing has been held, in the county in which it was held. Otherwise the application shall be made in the county where the adverse party resides or has a place of business or, if he has no residence or place of business in this

State, to the court of any county. All subsequent applications shall be made to the court hearing the initial application unless the court otherwise directs.

Section 19: Appeals

(a) An appeal may be taken from:

(1) An order denying an application to compel arbitration under Section 2;

(2) An order granting an application to stay arbitration made under Section 2(b);

(3) An order confirming or denying confirmation of an award;

(4) An order modifying or correcting an award;

(5) An order vacating an award without directing a rehearing; or

(6) A judgment or decree entered pursuant to the provisions of this act.

(b) The appeal shall be taken in the manner and to the same extent as from orders or judgments in a civil action.

Section 20: Act Not Retroactive

This act applies only to agreements made subsequent to the taking effect of this act.

Section 21: Uniformity of Interpretation

This act shall be so construed as to effectuate its general purpose to make uniform the law of those states which enact it.

Section 22: Constitutionality

If any provision of this act or the application thereof to any person or circumstance is held invalid, the invalidity shall not affect other provisions or application of the act which can be given without the invalid provision or application, and to this end the provisions of the act are severable.

Section 23: Short Title

This act may be cited as the Uniform Arbitration Act.

Section 24: Repeal

All acts or parts of acts which are inconsistent with the provisions of this act are hereby repealed.

Section 25: Time of Taking Effect

This act shall take effect on [date].

APPENDIX 16:

NATIONAL DIRECTORY OF DISPUTE RESOLUTION SERVICES

STATE	ORGANIZATION	ADDRESS	TELEPHONE NUMBER
ALABAMA	BETTER BUSINESS BUREAU, INC.	1214 SOUTH 20TH STREET BIRMINGHAM, AL 35202	205-933-2893
ALASKA	BETTER BUSINESS BUREAU OF ALASKA	3380 C STREET SUITE 103 ANCHORAGE, AK 99503	907-562-2824
ARIZONA	COMMUNITY MEDIATION PROGRAM	PO BOX 26504 TUCSON, AZ 85726	602-323-1706

STATE	ORGANIZATION	ADDRESS	TELEPHONE NUMBER
ARKANSAS	ARKANSAS CONSUMER PROTECTION PROGRAM	400 TOWER BUILDING FOURTH AND CENTER STREETS LITTLE ROCK, AR 72201	501-682-2341
CALIFORNIA	LOS ANGELES COUNTY BAR ASSOCIATION DISPUTE RESOLUTION SERVICE	617 SOUTH OLIVE STREET LOS ANGELES, CA 90014	213-627-2727
CALIFORNIA	STATE DEPARTMENT OF CONSUMER AFFAIRS CONSUMER ASSISTANCE OFFICE	1020 N STREET ROOM 500 SACRAMENTO, CA 95818	916-445-1254
CALIFORNIA	CALIFORNIA COMMUNITY DISPUTE SERVICES	445 BUSH STREET 5TH FLOOR SAN FRANCISCO, CA 94108	415-434-2200
COLORADO	OFFICE OF CONSUMER PROTECTION	1525 SHERMAN STREET ROOM 215 DENVER, CO 80203	303-866-5168
CONNECTICUT	WATERBURY SUPERIOR COURT MEDIATION PROGRAM	28 GRAND STREET HARTFORD, CT 06106	860-566-8187
DELAWARE	MEDIATION UNIT OF THE DELAWARE FAMILY COURT	PO BOX 2359 WILMINGTON, DE 19899	302-571-2270
DISTRICT OF COLUMBIA	CIVIL ARBITRATION PROGRAM	D.C. SUPERIOR COURT CIVIL DIVISION 500 INDIANA AVENUE, NW WASHINGTON, DC 20001	202-879-1680
DISTRICT OF COLUMBIA	FEDERAL MEDIATION AND CONCILIATION SERVICE	2100 K STREET, NW WASHINGTON, DC 20427	202-653-5300

STATE	ORGANIZATION	ADDRESS	TELEPHONE NUMBER
FLORIDA	METRO MEDIATION SERVICES	1500 NW 12TH AVENUE ROOM 708 MIAMI, FL 33126	305-547-7885
GEORGIA	GOVERNOR'S OFFICE OF CONSUMER AFFAIRS	TWO MARTIN LUTHER KING DRIVE SUITE 356-EAST TOWER ATLANTA, GA 30334	404-656-1760
HAWAII	PROGRAM ON ALTERNATIVE DISPUTE RESOLUTION	PO BOX 2560 HONOLULU, HI 96804	808-548-3080
IDAHO	IDAHO HUMAN RIGHTS COMMISSION	450 WEST STATE STREET BOISE, ID 83720	208-334-2873
ILLINOIS	ILLINOIS CONSUMER PROTECTION DIVISION	500 SOUTH SECOND SPRINGFIELD, IL 62706	217-782-9011
INDIANA	INDIANA CONSUMER PROTECTION DIVISION	219 STATE HOUSE INDIANAPOLIS, IN 46204	317-232-6203
IOWA	IOWA ATTORNEY GENERAL'S OFFICE	1300 EAST WALNUT DES MOINES, IA 50319	515-281-5926
KANSAS	DISPUTE RESOLUTION SERVICES	465 SOUTH PARKER SUITE 103 OLATHE, KS 66061	913-764-8585
KENTUCKY	PRETRIAL SERVICES	514 WEST LIBERTY STREET SUITE 105 LOUISVILLE, KY 40212	502-588-4142

STATE	ORGANIZATION	ADDRESS	TELEPHONE NUMBER
LOUISIANA	BETTER BUSINESS BUREAU	1401 NORTH MARKET STREET SHREVEPORT, LA 71107	318-221-8352
MAINE	COURT MEDIATION SERVICE	PO BOX 66 D.T.S PORTLAND, ME 04112	207-879-4700
MARYLAND	MARYLAND CONSUMER-BUSINESS BINDING ARBITRATION PROGRAM	138 EAST ANTIETAM STREET SUITE 210 HAGERSTOWN, MD 21740	301-791-4780
MARYLAND	U.S. DEPARTMENT OF JUSTICE COMMUNITY RELATIONS SERVICE	5550 FRIENDSHIP BOULEVARD SUITE 330 CHEVY CHASE, MD 20815	301-492-5948
MASSACHUSETTS	FACE-TO-FACE MEDIATION PROGRAM	131 TREMONT STREET BOSTON, MA 02111	617-727-2200
MASSACHUSETTS	Massachusetts BOARD OF CONCILIATION AND ARBITRATION	100 CAMBRIDGE STREET ROOM 1105 BOSTON, MA 02202	617-727-3466
MICHIGAN	CONSUMER PROTECTION DIVISION	690 LAW BUILDING 525 WEST OTTAWA STREET LANSING, MI 48913	517-373-1140
MINNESOTA	ACROSS THE BOARD MEDIATION/ARBITRATION AND BETTER BUSINESS BUREAU AUTOLINE PROGRAM	2706 GANNON ROAD ST. PAUL, MN 55116	612-646-4637
MINNESOTA	CONSUMER SERVICES DIVISION	117 UNIVERSITY AVENUE ROOM 124 ST. PAUL, MN 55155	612-296-3353

STATE	ORGANIZATION	ADDRESS	TELEPHONE NUMBER
MISSISSIPPI	BETTER BUSINESS BUREAU OF MISSISSIPPI	510 GEORGE STREET SUITE 107 JACKSON, MS 39202	601-948-8222
MISSOURI	BETTER BUSINESS BUREAU OF SOUTHWEST MISSOURI	205 PARK CENTRAL EAST SUITE 509 SPRINGFIELD, MO 65806,	417-862-9231
NEBRASKA	BETTER BUSINESS BUREAU	719 NORTH 48TH STREET LINCOLN, NB 68504	402-467-5261
NEVADA	DIVISION OF CONSUMER AFFAIRS	2601 EAST SAHARA AVENUE SUITE 247 LAS VEGAS, NV 89104	702-386-5293
NEW HAMPSHIRE	NEW HAMPSHIRE MEDIATION PROGRAM	33 STICKNEY AVENUE CONCORD, NH 03301	603-224-8043
NEW JERSEY	OFFICE OF CONSUMER PROTECTION	1100 RAYMOND BOULEVARD NEWARK, NJ 07102	201-648-3622
NEW JERSEY	CENTER FOR PUBLIC DISPUTE RESOLUTION	RICHARD J. HUGHES JUSTICE COMPLEX 25 MARKET STREET, CN 850 TRENTON, NJ 08625	609-292-1773
NEW MEXICO	NEW MEXICO CENTER FOR DISPUTE RESOLUTION	510 SECOND STREET, NW SUITE 209 ALBUQUERQUE, NM 87102	505-247-0571

STATE	ORGANIZATION	ADDRESS	TELEPHONE NUMBER
NEW YORK	COMMUNITY DISPUTE RESOLUTION CENTER	ALFRED E. SMITH BUILDING FIRST FLOOR ALBANY, NY 12225	518-473-4160
NEW YORK	CITY OF NEW YORK DEPARTMENT OF CONSUMER AFFAIRS	80 LAFAYETTE STREET NEW YORK, NY 10013	212-577-0111
NORTH CAROLINA	DISPUTE SETTLEMENT CENTER OF DURHAM INC.	PO BOX 2321 DURHAM, NC 27702	919-490-6777
NORTH DAKOTA	FEE ARBITRATION PANEL	PO BOX 2136 BISMARCK, ND 58502	701-255-1404
OHIO	BETTER BUSINESS BUREAU	425 JEFFERSON AVENUE TOLEDO OH 43604	419-241-6276
OHIO	COMMUNITY MEDIATION SERVICES OF CENTRAL OHIO	2504 SULLIVAN AVENUE COLUMBUS, OH 43204	614-276-7837
OKLAHOMA	EARLY SETTLEMENT PROGRAM	600 CIVIC CENTER ROOM 134 TULSA, OK 74103	918-596-7786
OREGON	NEIGHBORHOOD MEDIATION CENTER	4815 N.E. SEVENTH AVENUE PORTLAND, OR 97211	503-243-7320
PENNSYLVANIA	DISPUTE RESOLUTION PROGRAM	PHILADELPHIA MUNICIPAL COURT CITY HALL ANNEX ROOM 1005 PHILADELPHIA, PA 19107	215-686-2973

STATE	ORGANIZATION	ADDRESS	TELEPHONE NUMBER
PENNSYLVANIA	PITTSBURGH MEDIATION CENTER	7101 HAMILTON AVENUE PITTSBURGH, PA 15208	412-371-1231
RHODE ISLAND	BETTER BUSINESS BUREAU OF RHODE ISLAND INC.	100 BIGNALL STREET WARWICK, RI 02887	
SOUTH CAROLINA	OFFICE OF EXECUTIVE POLICY AND PROGRAMS	1205 PENDLETON STREET COLUMBIAM SC 29201	803-734-0457
SOUTH DAKOTA	DIVISION OF CONSUMER AFFAIRS	STATE CAPITOL BUILDING 500 EAST CAPITOL PIERRE, SD 57501	605-773-4400
TENNESSEE	TENNESSEE DIVISION OF CONSUMER AFFAIRS	500 JAMES ROBERTSON PARKWAY FIFTH FLOOR NASHVILLE, TN 37219	615-741-4737
TEXAS	DISPUTE MEDIATION SERVICE OF DALLAS INC.	3310 LIVE OAK SUITE 202-LB9 DALLAS, TX 75204	214-754-0022
TEXAS	DISPUTE RESOLUTION CENTER	301 SAN JACINTO SUITE 315 HOUSTON, TX 77001	713-221-6222
UTAH	DIVISION OF CONSUMER PROTECTION	160 EAST 300 SOUTH SALT LAKE CITY, UT 84145	801-530-6601
VERMONT	DISPUTE RESOLUTION CLINIC OF WOODBURY COLLEGE	659 ELM STREET MONTPELIER, VT 05602	802-229-0516

STATE	ORGANIZATION	ADDRESS	TELEPHONE NUMBER
VIRGINIA	DISPUTE RESOLUTION CENTER	701 EAST FRANKLIN STREET SUITE 712 RICHMOND, VA 23219	804-343-7355
WASHINGTON	BETTER BUSINESS BUREAU OF WASHINGTON	333 S.W. FIFTH AVENUE PORTLAND, OR 97204	503-226-3981
WISCONSIN	OFFICE OF CONSUMER PROTECTION	123 WEST WASHINGTON AVENUE ROOM 170 MADISON, WI 53707	608-266-1852
WYOMING	BETTER BUSINESS BUREAU	2144 SAGE AVENUE CASPER, WY 82604	307-268-2616

Note: This directory contains the larger state-wide dispute resolution programs handling a variety of types of cases in each state listed. There are many smaller dispute resolution programs conducted by various organizations serving specified geographical regions and more particularized caseloads within each state. For a more detailed list, please consult the source.

Source: Dispute Resolution Program Directory, American Bar Association, 750 N. Lake Shore Drive, Chicago, IL 60611 (Tel): 312-988-5000/ (Fax): 312-988-5568.

APPENDIX 17:
NATIONAL DIRECTORY OF AMERICAN ARBITRATION ASSOCIATION (AAA) OFFICES

STATE	ADDRESS	TELEPHONE NUMBER	FAX NUMBER
ARIZONA	333 EAST OSBORN ROAD, SUITE 310 PHOENIX, AZ 85012-2365	602-234-0950	602-230-2151
CALIFORNIA	2030 MAIN STREET, SUITE 1650 IRVINE, CA 92614-7240	949-251-9840	949-251-9842
CALIFORNIA	3055 WILSHIRE BOULEVARD, FLOOR 7 LOS ANGELES, CA 90010-1108	213-383-6516	213-386-2251

STATE	ADDRESS	TELEPHONE NUMBER	FAX NUMBER
CALIFORNIA	600 B STREET, SUITE 1450 SAN DIEGO, CA 92101-4586	619-239-3051	619-239-3807
CALIFORNIA	225 BUSH STREET, FLOOR 18 SAN FRANCISCO, CA 94104-4207	415-981-3901	415-781-8426
COLORADO	1660 LINCOLN STREET, SUITE 2150 DENVER, CO 80264-2101	303-831-0823	303-832-3626
CONNECTICUT	111 FOUNDERS PLAZA, FLOOR 17 EAST HARTFORD, CT 06108-3240	860-289-3993	860-282-0459
DISTRICT OF COLUMBIA	601 PENNSYLVANIA AVENUE N.W. SUITE 700 WASHINGTON, DC 20004-2676	202-737-9191	202-737-9099
FLORIDA	799 BRICKELL PLAZA, SUITE 600 MIAMI, FL 33131-2808	305-358-7777	305-358-4931
FLORIDA	315 EAST ROBINSON STREET, SUITE 290 ORLANDO, FL 32801-2742	407-648-1185	407-649-8668
GEORGIA	2200 CENTURY PARKWAY, SUITE 300 ATLANTA, GA 30345-3203	404-325-0101	404-325-8034
ILLINOIS	225 NORTH MICHIGAN AVENUE, SUITE 2527 CHICAGO, IL 60601-7601	312-616-6560	312-819-0404
LOUISIANA	2810 ENERGY CENTRE 1100 POYDRAS STREET NEW ORLEANS, LA 70163-2810	504-522-8781	504-561-8041

STATE	ADDRESS	TELEPHONE NUMBER	FAX NUMBER
MASSACHUSETTS	133 FEDERAL STREET, FLOOR 10 BOSTON, MA 02110-1703	617-451-6600	617-451-0763
MICHIGAN	ONE TOWNE SQUARE, SUITE 1600 SOUTHFIELD, MI 48076-3728	248-352-5500	248-352-3147
MINNESOTA	700 PILLSBURY CENTER 200 SOUTH SIXTH STREET MINNEAPOLIS, MN 55402-1092	612-332-6545	612-342-2334
MISSOURI	1101 WALNUT STREET, SUITE 903 KANSAS CITY, MO 64106-2110	816-221-6401	816-471-5264
MISSOURI	ONE MERCANTILE CENTER, SUITE 2512 ST. LOUIS, MO 63101-1614	314-621-7175	314-621-3730
NEVADA	5440 WEST SAHARA AVENUE, SUITE 206 LAS VEGAS, NV 89146-0365	702-252-4071	702-252-4073
NEW JERSEY	265 DAVIDSON AVENUE, SUITE 140 SOMERSET, NJ 08873-4159	732-560-9560	732-560-8850
NEW YORK (CORPORATE HEADQUARTERS)	335 MADISON AVENUE, FLOOR 10 NEW YORK, NY 10017-4605	212-716-5800	212-716-5905
NEW YORK (INTERNATIONAL CENTER FOR DISPUTE RESOLUTION)	1633 BROADWAY, FLOOR 10 NEW YORK, NY 10019-6708	212-484-4181	212-246-7274
NEW YORK	666 OLD COUNTRY ROAD, SUITE 603 GARDEN CITY, NY 11530-2004	516-222-1660	516-745-6447

STATE	ADDRESS	TELEPHONE NUMBER	FAX NUMBER
NEW YORK	140 WEST 51ST STREET NEW YORK, NY 10020-1203	212-484-4000	212-307-4387
NEW YORK	65 BROADWAY NEW YORK, NY 10006	917-438-1500	917-438-1600
NEW YORK	115 EAST JEFFERSON STREET, SUITE 401 SYRACUSE, NY 13202-2595	315-472-5483	315-472-0966
NEW YORK	399 KNOLLWOOD ROAD, SUITE 116 WHITE PLAINS, NY 10603-1916	914-946-1119	914-946-2661
NORTH CAROLINA	6100 FAIRVIEW ROAD, SUITE 300 CHARLOTTE, NC 28210-3277	704-347-0200	704-347-2804
OHIO	525 VINE STREET, SUITE 1070 CINCINNATI, OH 45202-3123	513-241-8434	513-241-8437
OHIO	25050 COUNTRY CLUB BOULEVARD, SUITE 200 NORTH OLMSTED, OH 44070	440-716-2220	440-716-2221
PENNSYLVANIA	230 SOUTH BROAD STREET, FLOOR 12 PHILADELPHIA, PA 19102-4199	215-732-5260	215-732-5002
PENNSYLVANIA	FOUR GATEWAY CENTER, ROOM 1939 PITTSBURGH, PA 15222-1207	412-261-3617	412-261-6055
TENNESSEE	211 SEVENTH AVENUE NORTH, SUITE 300 NASHVILLE, TN 37219-1823	615-256-5857	615-244-8570

STATE	ADDRESS	TELEPHONE NUMBER	FAX NUMBER
TEXAS	1750 TWO GALLERIA TOWER 13455 NOEL ROAD DALLAS, TX 75240-6636	972-702-8222	972-490-9008
TEXAS	1001 FANNIN STREET, SUITE 1005 HOUSTON, TX 77002-6708	713-739-1302	713-739-1702
UTAH	645 SOUTH 200TH STREET EAST, SUITE 203 SALT LAKE CITY, UT 84111-3834	801-531-9748	801-323-9624
VIRGINIA	707 EAST MAIN STREET, SUITE 1610 RICHMOND, VA 23219-2803	804-649-4838	804-698-7365
WASHINGTON	1020 ONE UNION SQUARE 600 UNIVERSITY STREET SEATTLE, WA 98101-4111	206-622-6435	206-343-5679

Source: American Arbitration Association\tab 2000.

APPENDIX 18:
GENERAL RELEASE OF CLAIMS

JANE DOE, 100 Main Street, New York, NY 10001, ("Releasor"), for the sole consideration of the sum of TEN THOUSAND ($10,000.00) DOLLARS, and upon receipt thereof, does hereby release, acquit and forever discharge XYZ SUPERMARKET, 200 Main Street, New York, NY 10001, ("Releasee"), its successors and assigns, heirs, executors and administrators, of and from all causes of action, claims, demands, damages, costs, loss of services, expenses and judgments, which we now have or may have hereafter because of any matter or thing which may have happened, developed or occurred before the signing of this release.

This settlement is compensation for personal injuries sustained on or about November 15, 1999, filed under ABC Insurance Carrier Claim #1234567.

The words "RELEASOR" and "RELEASEE" includes all releasors and all releasees under this RELEASE. This RELEASE may not be changed orally.

In Witness Whereof, the RELEASOR has hereunto signed her name this 27th day of March, 2000.

BY: Jane Doe, Releasor

GLOSSARY

Accrue	To occur or come into existence.
Action at Law	A judicial proceeding whereby one party prosecutes another for a wrong done.
Actionable	Giving rise to a cause of action.
Actionable Negligence	The breach or nonperformance of a legal duty through neglect or carelessness, resulting in damage or injury to another.
Actual Damages	Actual damages are those damages directly referable to the breach or tortious act, and which can be readily proven to have been sustained, and for which the injured party should be compensated as a matter of right.
Ad Damnum Clause	The clause in a complaint which sets forth the amount of damages demanded.
Adjudication	The determination of a controversy and pronouncement of judgment.
Admissible Evidence	Evidence which may be received by a trial court to assist the trier of fact, either the judge or jury, in deciding a dispute.
Adversary	Opponent or litigant in a legal controversy or litigation.

Affirmative Defense In a pleading, a matter constituting a defense.

Agency The relationship between a principal and an agent who is employed by the principal, to perform certain acts dealing with third parties.

Agent One who represents another known as the principal.

Allegation Statement of the issue that the contributing party is prepared to prove.

Answer In a civil proceeding, the principal pleading on the part of the defendant in response to the plaintiff's complaint.

Appearance To come into court, personally or through an attorney, after being summoned.

Argument A discourse set forth for the purpose of establishing one's position in a controversy.

Assumption of Risk The legal doctrine that a plaintiff may not recover for an injury to which he assents.

Attorney In Fact An attorney-in-fact is an agent or representative of another given authority to act in that person's name and place pursuant to a document called a "power of attorney."

Battery The unlawful application of force to the person of another.

Breach of Contract The failure, without any legal excuse, to perform any promise which forms the whole or the part of a contract.

Breach of Duty In a general sense, any violation or omission of a legal or moral duty.

Burden of Proof The duty of a party to substantiate an allegation or issue to convince the trier of fact as to the truth of their claim.

Capacity	Capacity is the legal qualification concerning the ability of one to understand the nature and effects of one's acts.
Caption	The heading of a legal document which contains the name of the court, the index number assigned to the matter, and the names of the parties.
Cause of Action	The factual basis for bringing a lawsuit.
Child Abuse	Any form of cruelty to a child's physical, moral or mental well-being.
Child Protective Agency	A state agency responsible for the investigation of child abuse and neglect reports.
Circumstantial Evidence	Indirect evidence by which a principal fact may be inferred.
Compensatory Damages	Compensatory damages are those damages directly referable to a breach or tortious act, and which can be readily proven to have been sustained, and for which the injured party should be compensated as a matter of right.
Complaint	In a civil proceeding, the first pleading of the plaintiff setting out the facts on which the claim for relief is based.
Compromise and Settlement	An arrangement arrived at, either in court or out of court, for settling a dispute upon what appears to the parties to be equitable terms.
Conclusion of Fact	A conclusion reached by natural inference and based solely on the facts presented.
Conclusion of Law	A conclusion reached through the application of rules of law.
Conclusive Evidence	Evidence which is incontrovertible.

Contingency Fee   The fee charged by an attorney, which is dependent upon a successful outcome in the case, and is often agreed to be a percentage of the party's recovery.

Contribution   Sharing of a loss or payment among two or more parties.

Contributory Negligence   The act or omission amounting to want of ordinary care on the part of the complaining party which, concurring with the defendant's negligence, is the proximate cause of his or her injury.

Coroner   The public official whose responsibility it is to investigate the circumstances and causes of deaths which occur within his or her jurisdiction.

Costs   A sum payable by the losing party to the successful party for his or her expenses in prosecuting or defending a case.

Counterclaims   Counterdemands made by a respondent in his or her favor against a claimant. They are not mere answers or denials of the claimant's allegation.

Cross-claim   Claim litigated by co-defendants or co-plaintiffs, against each other, and not against a party on the opposing side of the litigation.

Court   The branch of government responsible for the resolution of disputes arising under the laws of the government.

Cross-Examination   The questioning of a witness by someone other than the one who called the witness to the stand concerning matters about which the witness testified during direct examination.

Damages   In general, damages refers to monetary compensation which the law awards to one who has been injured by the actions of another, such as in the case of tortious conduct or breach of contractual obligations.

Defendant	In a civil proceeding, the party responding to the complaint.
Defense	Opposition to the truth or validity of the plaintiff's claims.
Deposition	A method of pretrial discovery which consists of a statement of a witness under oath, taken in question and answer form as it would be in court, with opportunity given to the adversary to be present and cross-examine.
Discovery	Modern pretrial procedure by which one party gains information held by another party.
Duty	The obligation, to which the law will give recognition and effect, to conform to a particular standard of conduct toward another.
Expert Witness	A witness who has special knowledge about a certain subject, upon which he or she will testify, which knowledge is not normally possessed by the average person.
Eyewitness	A person who can testify about a matter because of his or her own presence at the time of the event.
Fact Finder	In a judicial or administrative proceeding, the person, or group of persons, that has the responsibility of determining the acts relevant to decide a controversy.
Finding	Decisions made by the court on issues of fact or law.
Foreseeability	A concept used to limit the liability of a party for the consequences of his acts to consequences that are within the scope of a foreseeable risk.

General Damages	General damages are those damages directly referable to the breach or tortious act and which can be readily proven to have been sustained, and for which the injured party should be compensated as a matter of right.
Guardian	A person who is entrusted with the management of the property and/or person of another who is incapable, due to age or incapacity, to administer their own affairs.
Implied Consent	Consent which is manifested by signs, actions or facts, or by inaction or silence, which raises a presumption that consent has been given.
Incapacity	Incapacity is a defense to breach of contract which refers to a lack of legal, physical or intellectual power to enter into a contract.
Infancy	The state of a person who is under the age of legal majority.
Informed Consent	The requirement that a patient be apprised of the nature and risks of a medical procedure before the physician can validly claim exemption from liability for battery, or from responsibility for medical complications.
Injury	Any damage done to another's person, rights, reputation or property.
Intentional Tort	A tort or wrong perpetrated by one who intends to do that which the law has declared wrong, as contrasted with negligence in which the tortfeasor fails to exercise that degree of care in doing what is otherwise permissible.
Judgment	A judgment is a final determination by a court of law concerning the rights of the parties to a lawsuit.
Jurisdiction	The power to hear and determine a case.

Jury	A group of individuals summoned to decide the facts in issue in a lawsuit.
Jury Trial	A trial during which the evidence is presented to a jury so that they can determine the issues of fact, and render a verdict based upon the law as it applies to their findings of fact.
Lay Witness	Any witness not testifying as an expert witness.
Legal Capacity	Referring to the legal capacity to sue, it is the requirement that a person bringing the lawsuit have a sound mind, be of lawful age, and be under no restraint or legal disability.
Medical Malpractice	The failure of a physician to exercise that degree of skill and learning commonly applied under all the circumstances in the community by the average prudent reputable professional in the same field.
Minor	A person who has not yet reached the age of legal competence, which is designated as 18 in most states.
Negligence	The failure to exercise the degree of care which a reasonable person would exercise given the same circumstances.
Negligence Per Se	Conduct, whether of action or omission, which may be declared and treated as negligence without any argument or proof as to the particular surrounding circumstances, because it is contrary to the law.
Non Obstante Verdicto (N.O.V.)	Latin for "notwithstanding the verdict." It refers to a judgment of the court which reverses the jury's verdict, based on the judge's determination that the verdict has no basis in law or is unsupported by the facts.

Objection	The process by which it is asserted that a particular question, or piece of evidence, is improper, and it is requested that the court rule upon the objectionable matter.
Pain and Suffering	Refers to damages recoverable against a wrongdoer which include physical or mental suffering.
Parens Patriae	Latin for "parent of his country." Refers to the role of the state as guardian of legally disabled individuals.
Parties	The disputants.
Plaintiff	In a civil proceeding, the one who initially brings the lawsuit.
Pleadings	Refers to plaintiff's complaint which sets forth the facts of the cause of action, and defendant's answer which sets forth the responses and defenses to the allegations contained in the complaint.
Power of Attorney	A legal document authorizing another to act on one's behalf.
Prima Facie Case	A case which is sufficient on its face, being supported by at least the requisite minimum of evidence, and being free from palpable defects.
Proximate Cause	That which, in a natural and continuous sequence, unbroken by any efficient intervening cause, produces injury, and without which the result would not have occurred.
Punitive Damages	Compensation in excess of compensatory damages which serves as a form of punishment to the wrongdoer who has exhibited malicious and willful misconduct.
Question of Fact	The fact in dispute which is the province of the trier of fact, i.e., the judge or jury, to decide.

Question of Law
The question of law which is the province of the judge to decide.

Release
A document signed by one party, releasing claims he or she may have against another party, usually as part of a settlement agreement.

Relief
The remedies afforded a complainant by the court.

Res Ipsa Loquitur
Literally, "the thing speaks for itself." Refers to an evidentiary rule which provides that negligence may be inferred from the fact that an accident occurred when such an occurrence would not ordinarily have happened in the absence of negligence, the cause of the occurrence was within the exclusive control of the defendant, and the plaintiff was in no way at fault.

Retainer Agreement
A contract between an attorney and the client stating the nature of the services to be rendered and the cost of the litigation.

Service of Process
The delivery of legal court documents, such as a complaint, to the defendant.

Settlement
An agreement by the parties to a dispute on a resolution of the claims, usually requiring some mutual action, such as payment of money in consideration of a release of claims.

Summons
A mandate requiring the appearance of the defendant in an action under penalty of having judgment entered against him for failure to do so.

Survival Statute
A statute that preserves for a decedent's estate a cause of action for infliction of pain and suffering and related damages suffered up to the moment of death.

Testimony
The sworn statement make by a witness in a judicial proceeding.

Tort	A private or civil wrong or injury, other than breach of contract, for which the court will provide a remedy in the form of an action for damages.
Tortfeasor	A wrong-doer.
Tortious Conduct	Wrongful conduct, whether of act or omission, of such a character as to subject the actor to liability under the law of torts.
Trial	The judicial procedure whereby disputes are determined based on the presentation of issues of law and fact. Issues of fact are decided by the trier of fact, either the judge or jury, and issues of law are decided by the judge.
Trial Court	The court of original jurisdiction over a particular matter.
Venue	The proper place for trial of a lawsuit.
Verdict	The definitive answer given by the jury to the court concerning the matters of fact committed to the jury for their deliberation and determination.
Verification	The confirmation of the authenticity of a document, such as an affidavit.
Vicarious Liability	In tort law, refers to the liability assessed against one party due to the actions of another party.
Ward	A person over whom a guardian is appointed to manage his or her affairs.
Wrongful Death Statute	A statute that creates a cause of action for any wrongful act, neglect, or default that causes death.

BIBLIOGRAPHY

Black's Law Dictionary, Fifth Edition. St. Paul, MN: West Publishing Company, 1979.

Eldridge, Burgess C. and Atwood, Sharon Personal Injury Paralegal. New York, NY: John Wiley & sons, Inc., 1992.

Gifis, Steven H. Barron's Law Dictionary, Second Edition. Woodbury, NY: Barron's Educational Series, Inc., 1984.

North, Steven E. Handling Your First Medical Malpractice Case: Fundamentals of Case Management. New York, NY: Practicing Law Institute, 1991.

King, Jr., Joseph H. The Law of Medical Malpractice. St. Paul, MN: West Publishing Co., 1977.

Phillips, Jerry J. Products Liability. St. Paul, MN: West Publishing Company, 1988.

Reis, Howard R. *Personal Injury and Product Liability Litigation*. Englewood Cliffs, NJ: Prentice-Hall, Inc., 1987.

Rojak, Lawrence N. *New York Insurance and Negligence Digest*. Costa Mesa, CA: James Publishing, Inc., 1999.

Rogers, James S. *Anatomy of a Personal Injury Lawsuit*. Washington, DC: ATLA Press, 1991.

Shayne, Neil T. *Winning the "Slip and Fall" Case*. New York, NY: Practicing Law Institute, 1989.

Turnbow, Charles E. *Slip & Fall Practice*. Costa Mesa, CA: James Publishing, Inc., 1999.

Shayne, Neil T. and Breenan, Lawrence J. *Evaluating and Settling a Personal Injury Case*. New York, NY: Practicing Law Institute, 1992.

Weitz, Harvey *The No-Fault Handbook*. New York, NY: The New York State Trial Lawyers Association, 1984.

For Reference

Not to be taken from this room